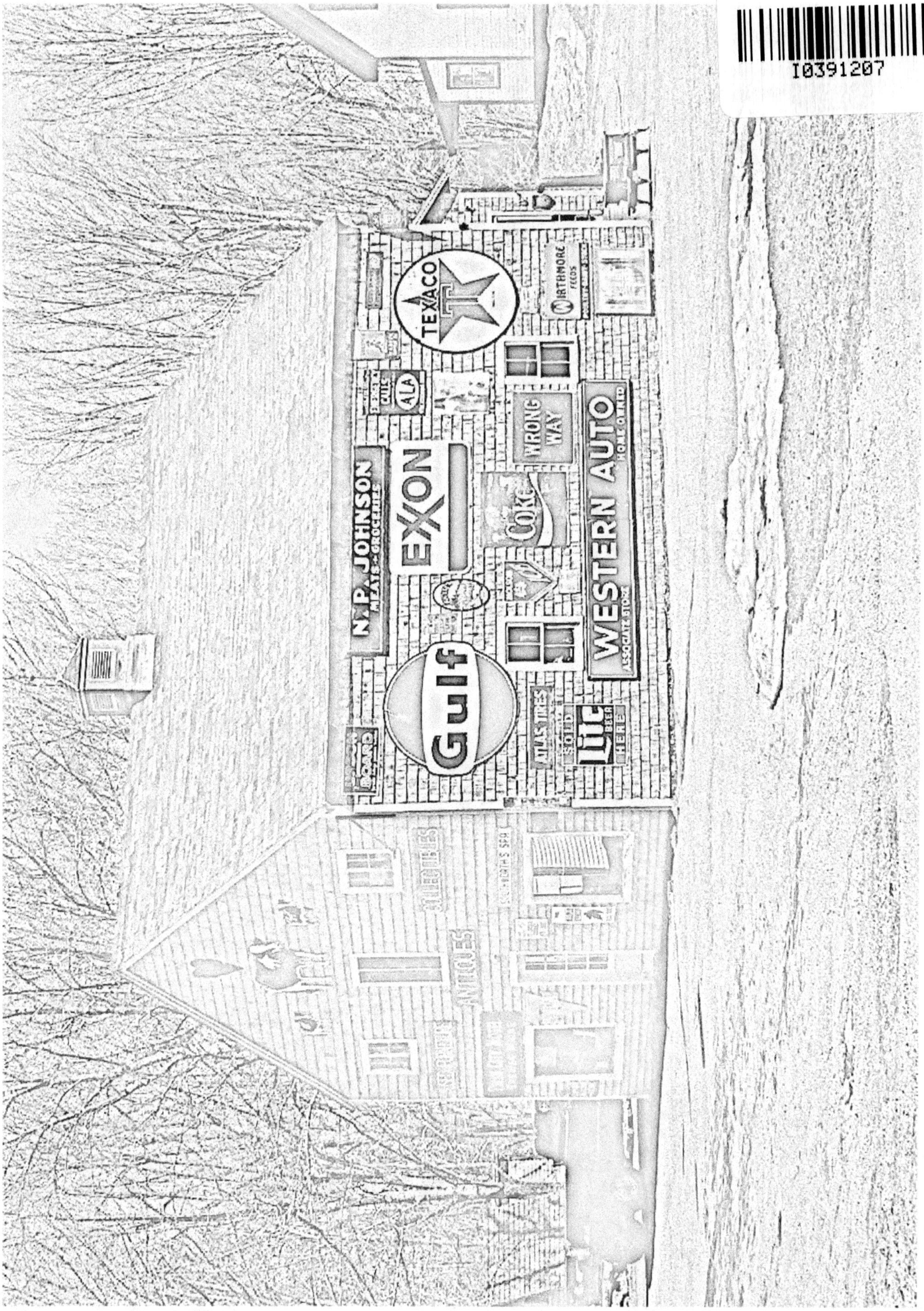
N. P. JOHNSON
MEATS - GROCERIES
EXXON
TEXACO
Gulf
WRONG WAY
Coke
WESTERN AUTO
HOME OWNED
ASSOCIATE STORE
ATLAS TIRES
SOLD HERE
Lite
ALA

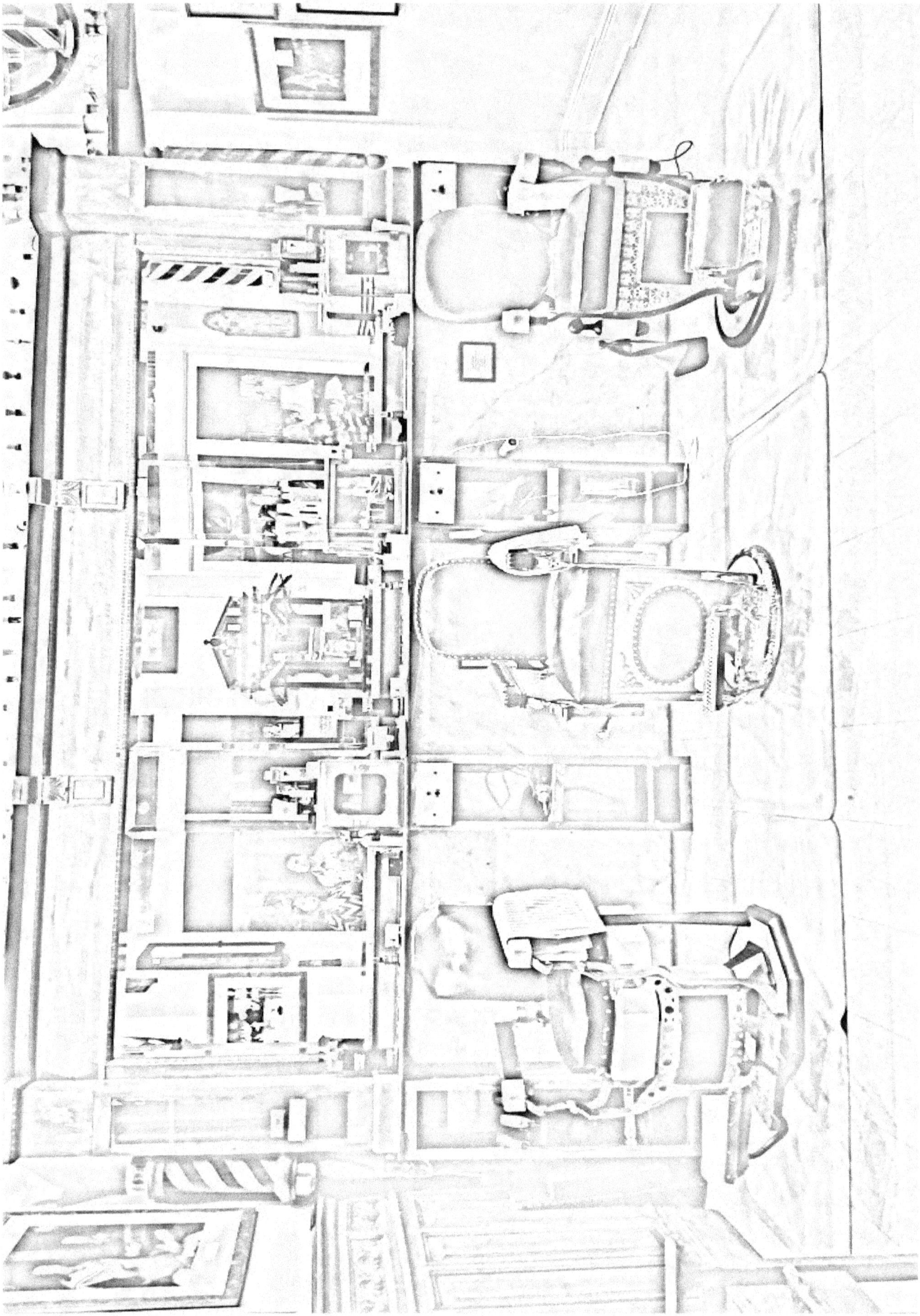

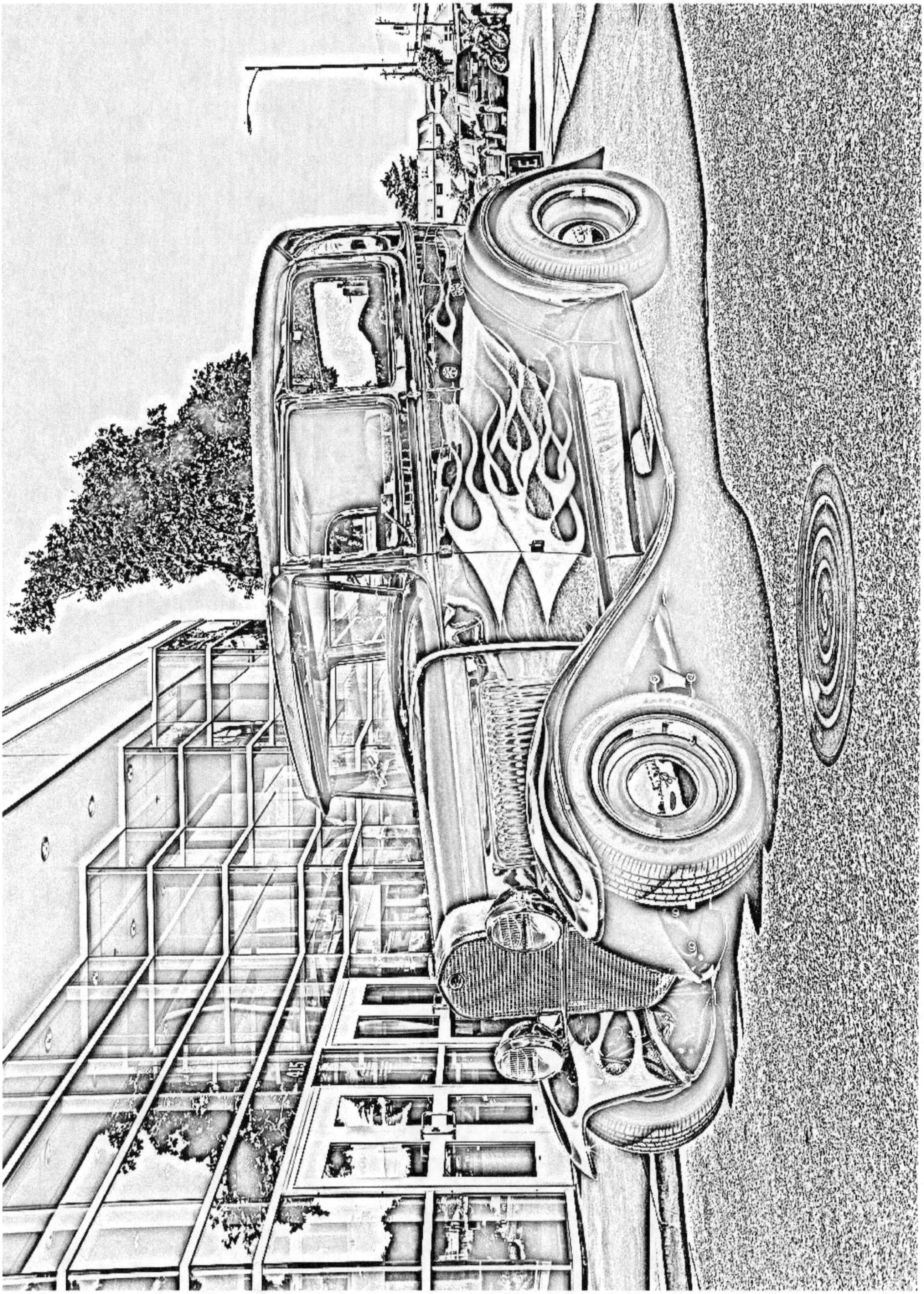

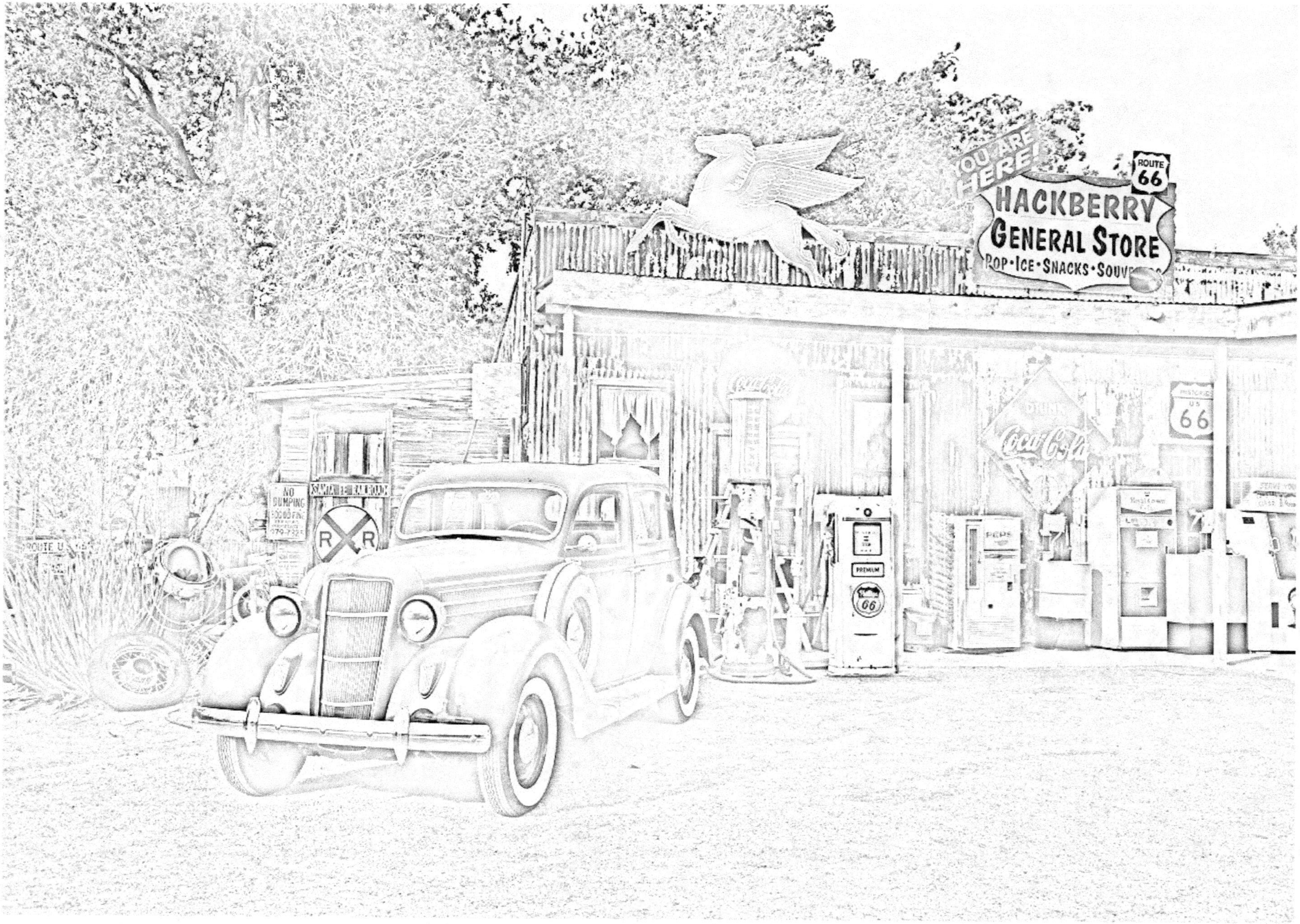
ROUTE 66
YOU ARE HERE!
HACKBERRY
GENERAL STORE
POP • ICE • SNACKS • SOUVE
NO DUMPING
SANTA FE RAILROAD
R X R
PREMIUM
66
Coca-Cola

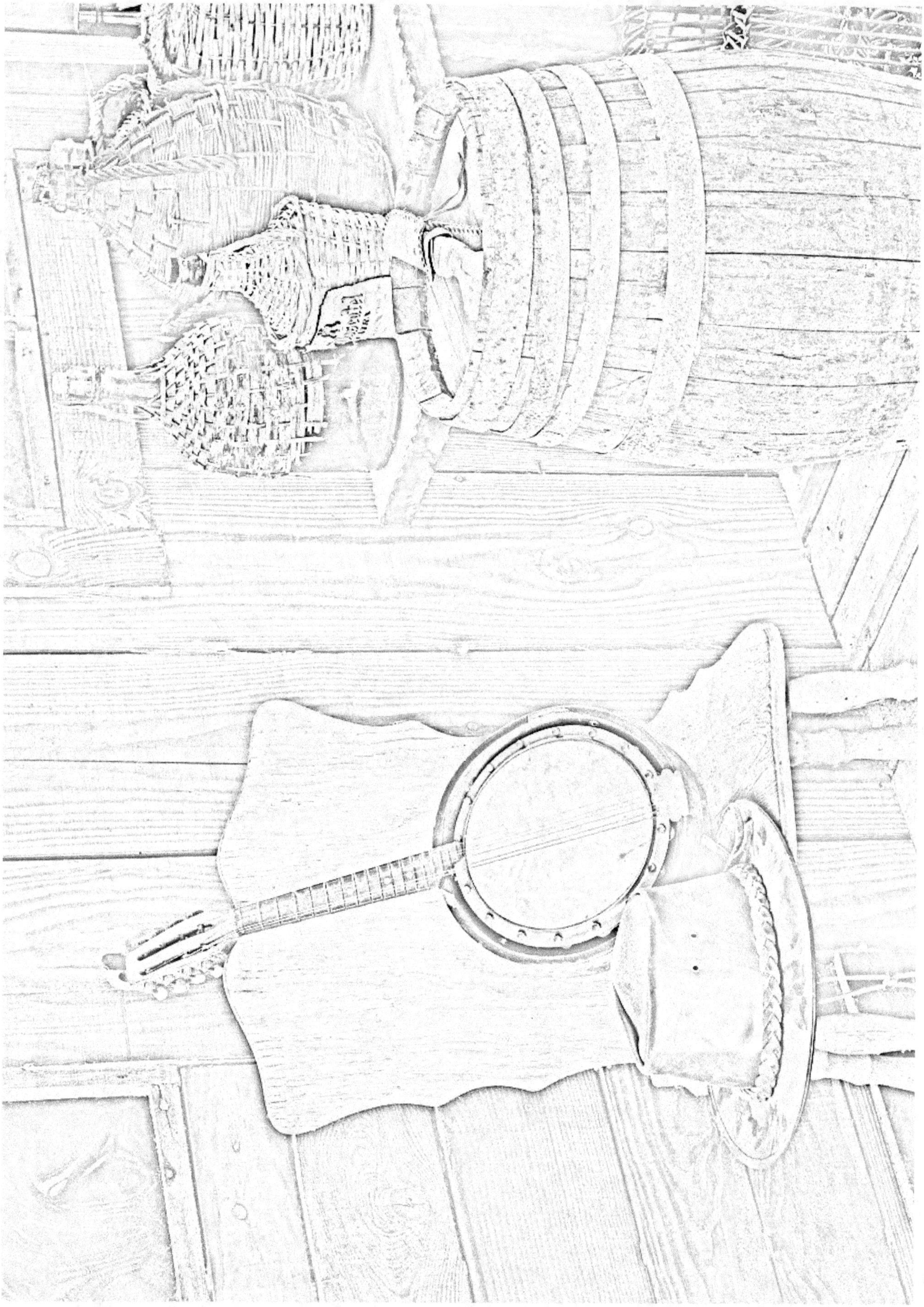

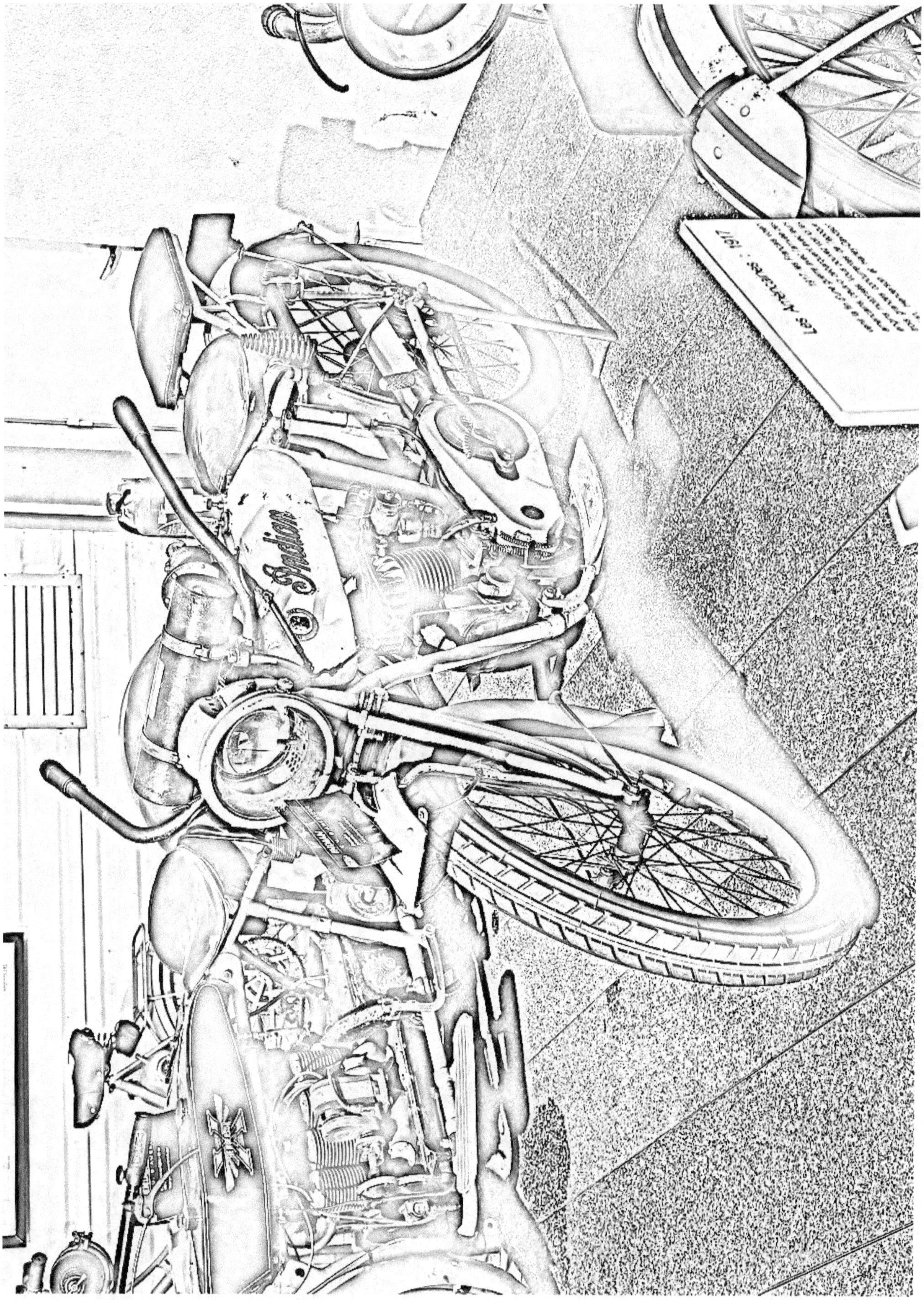
Indian

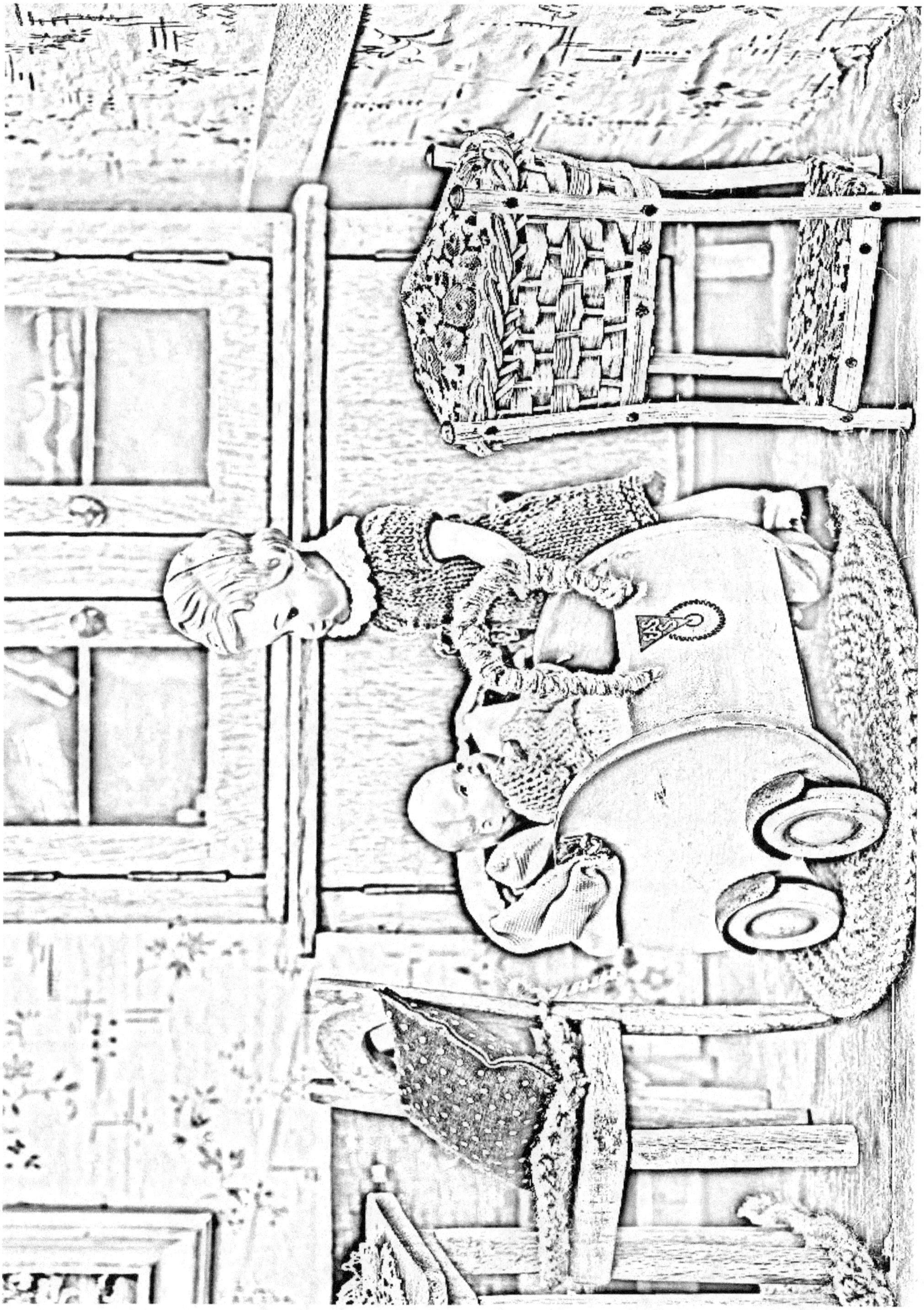

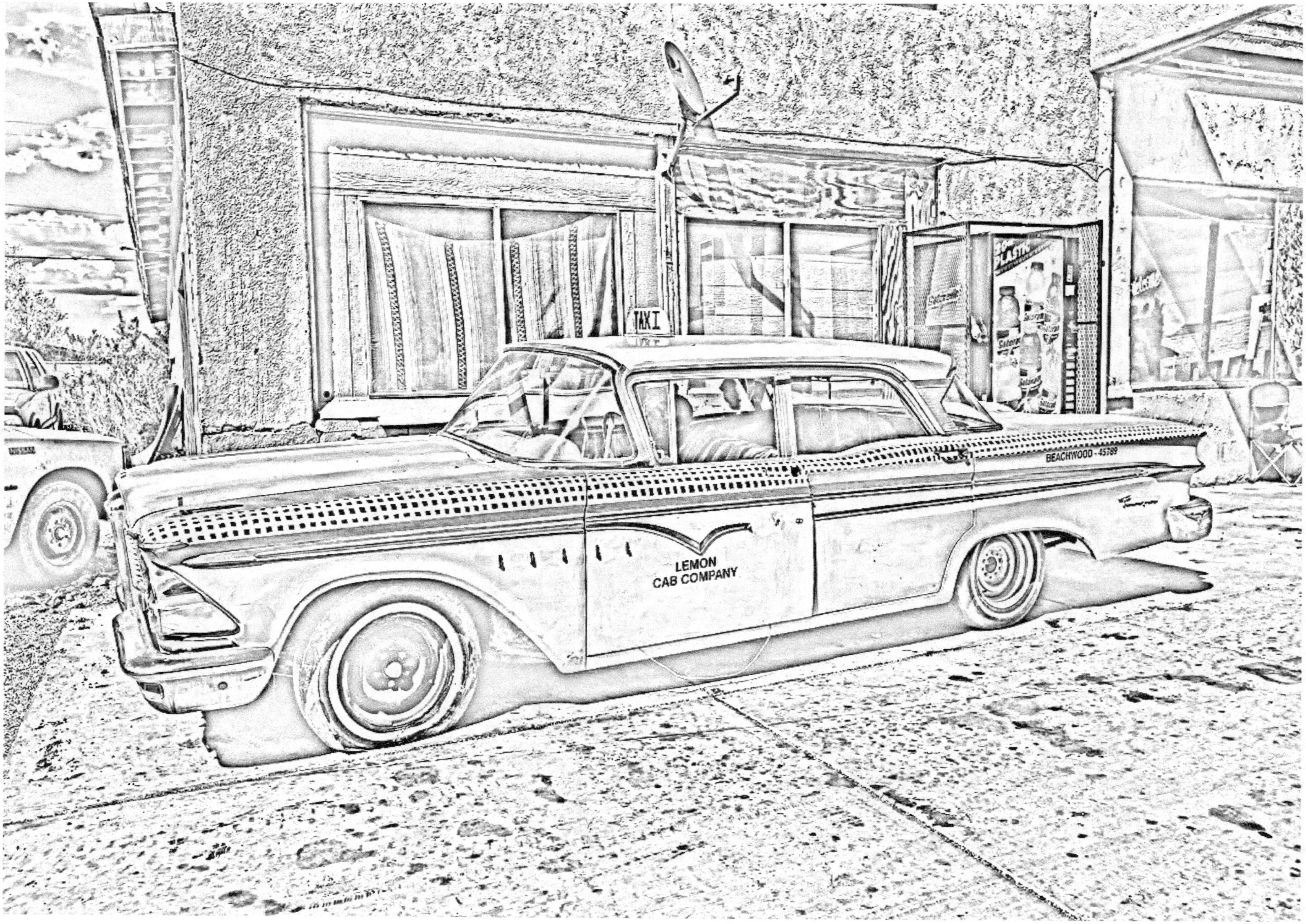

TAXI
LEMON
CAB COMPANY
BEACHWOOD - 45789

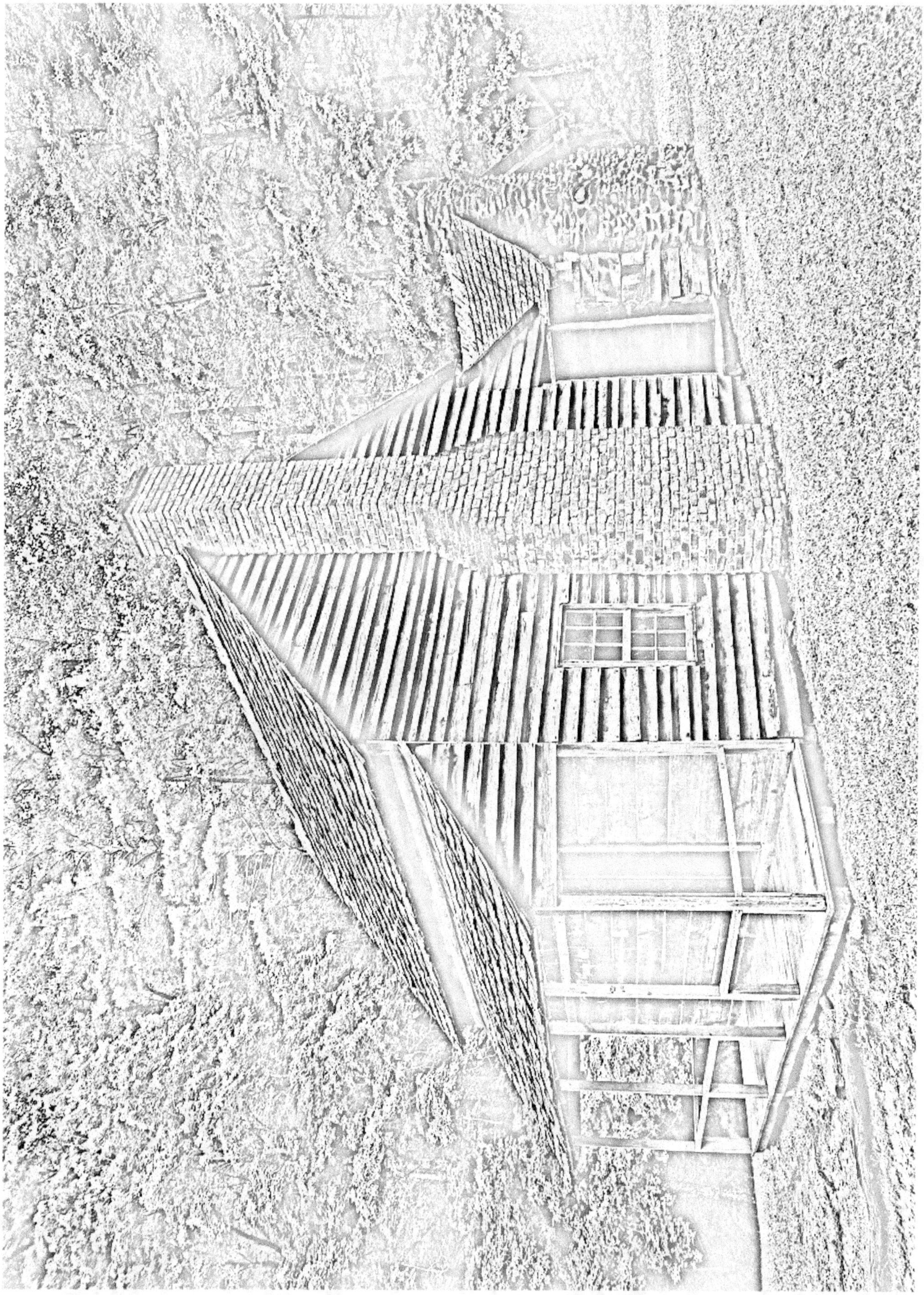

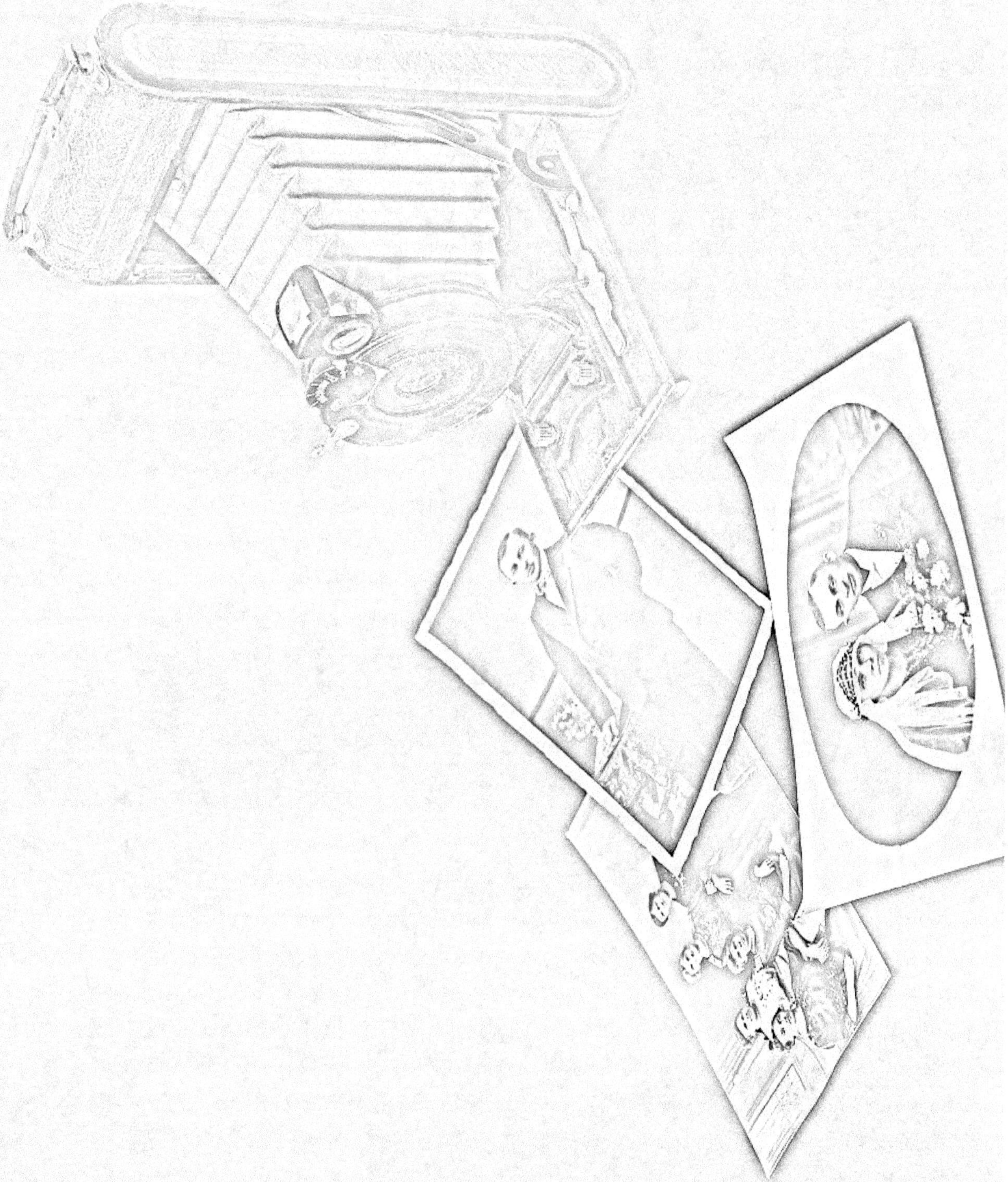

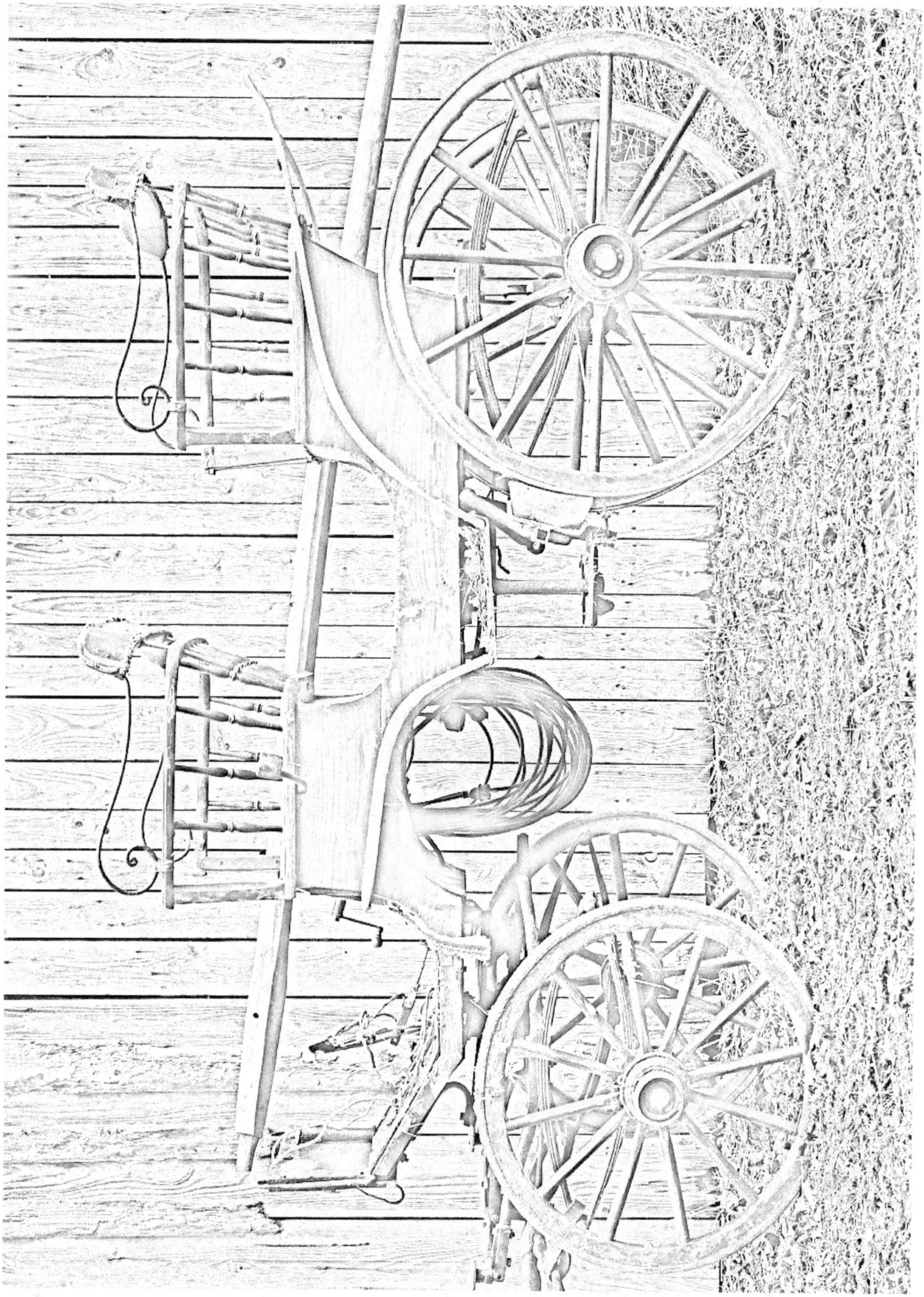

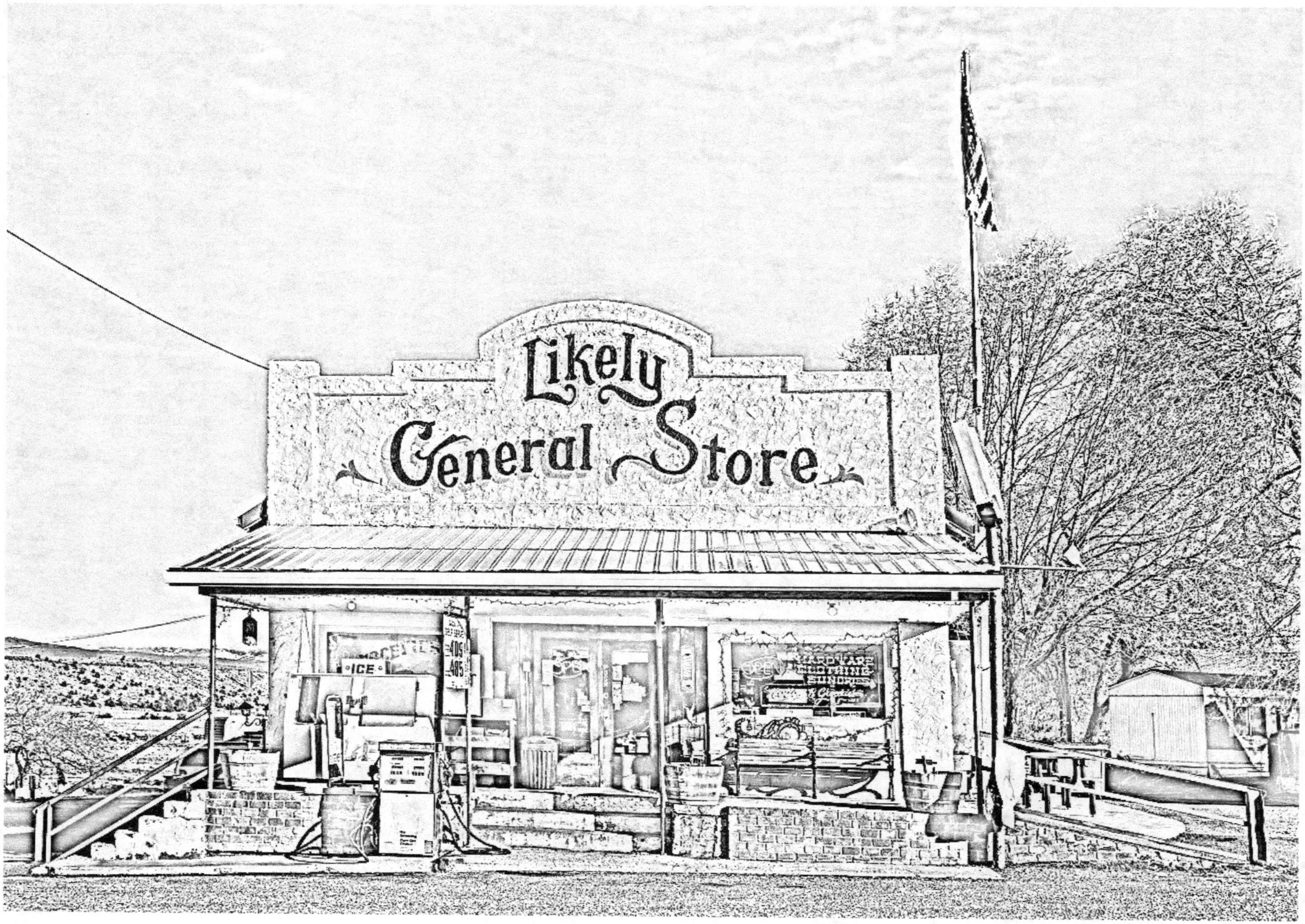
Likely
General Store
ICE

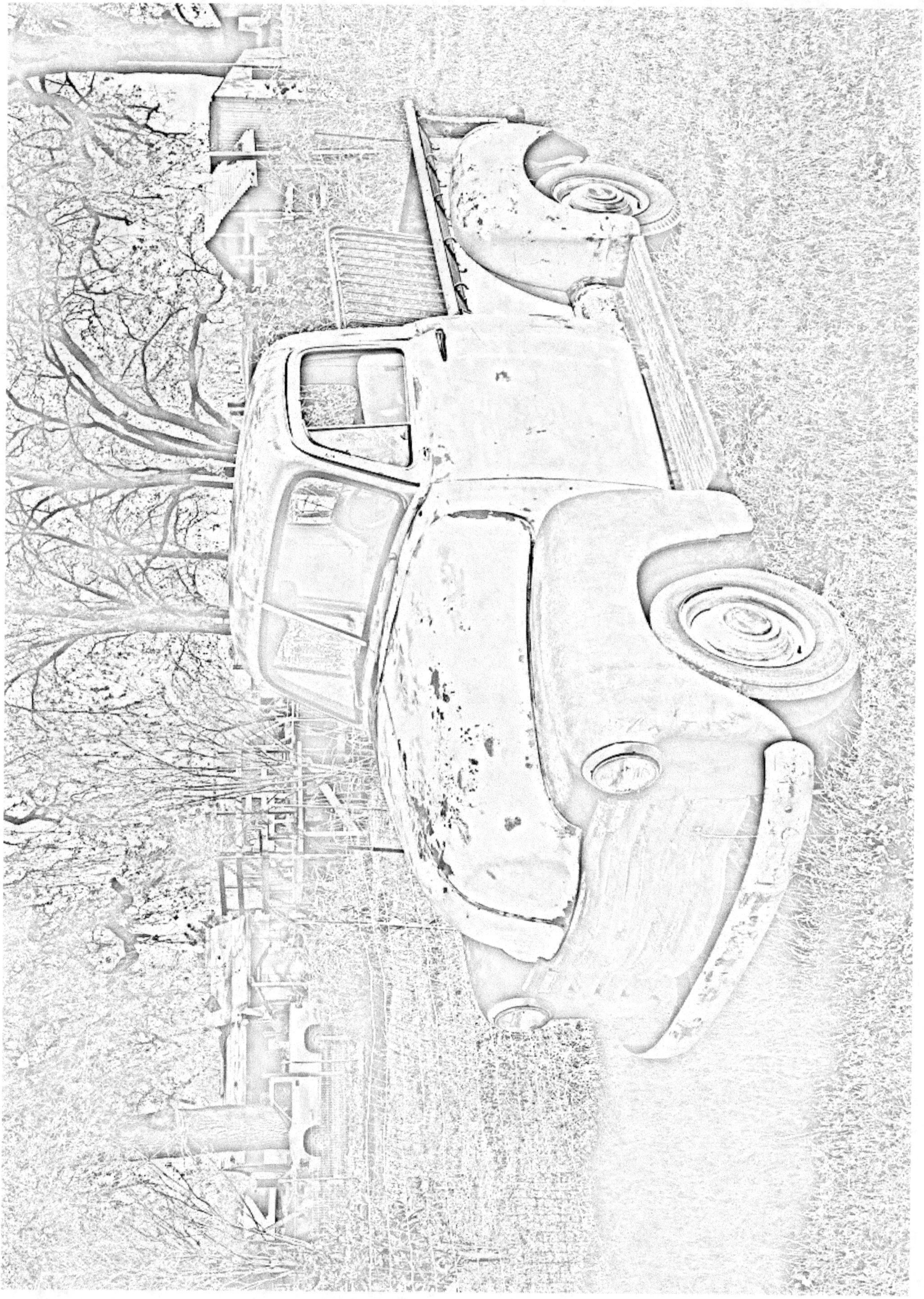

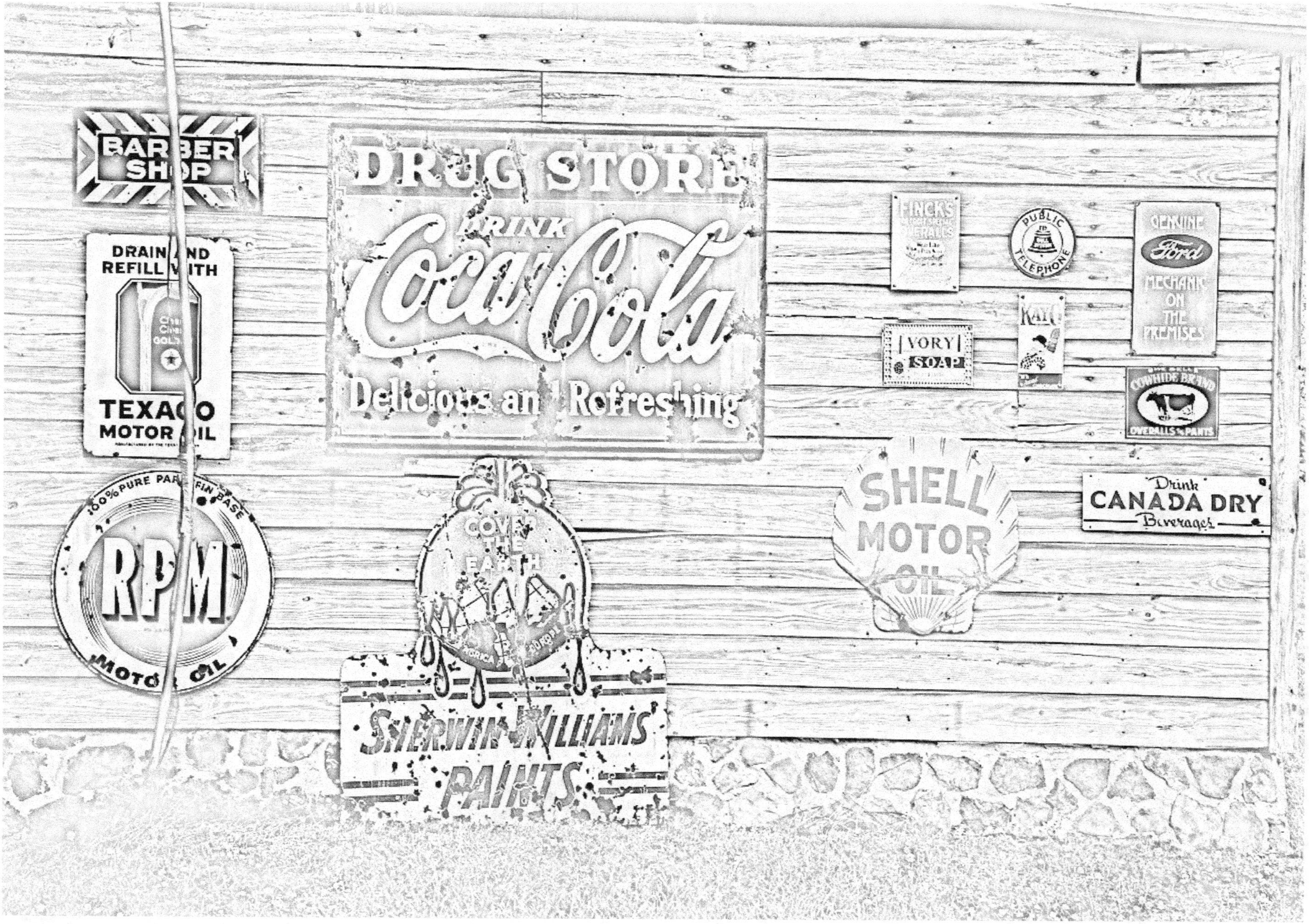
BARBER SHOP
DRAIN AND REFILL WITH
TEXACO MOTOR OIL
100% PURE PARAFFIN BASE
RPM
MOTOR OIL
DRUG STORE
DRINK
Coca-Cola
Delicious and Refreshing
COVER THE EARTH
SHERWIN-WILLIAMS
PAINTS
FINCKS
IVORY SOAP
PUBLIC TELEPHONE
GENUINE
Ford
MECHANIC ON THE PREMISES
COWHIDE BRAND
OVERALLS & PANTS
SHELL MOTOR OIL
Drink
CANADA DRY
Beverages

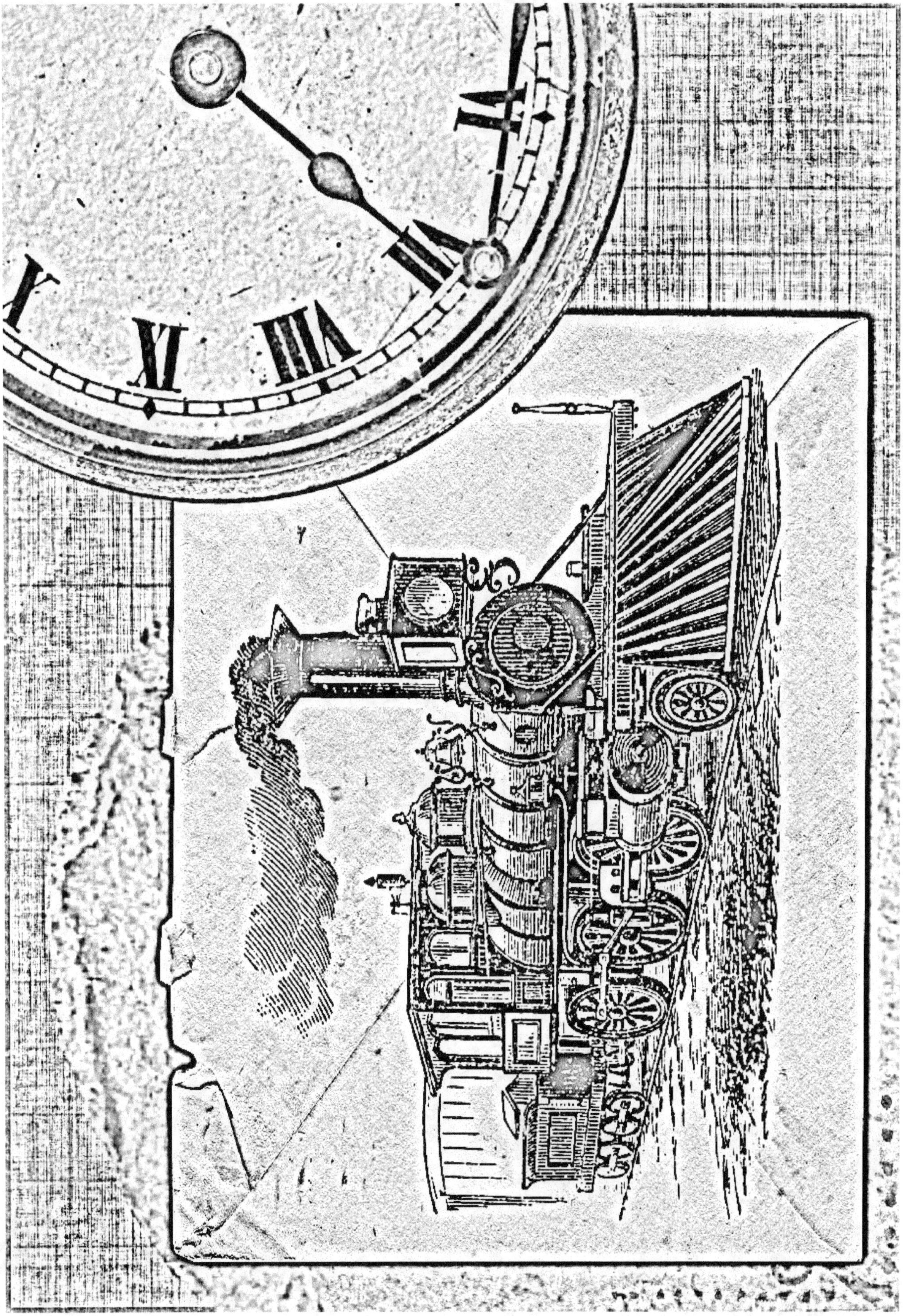

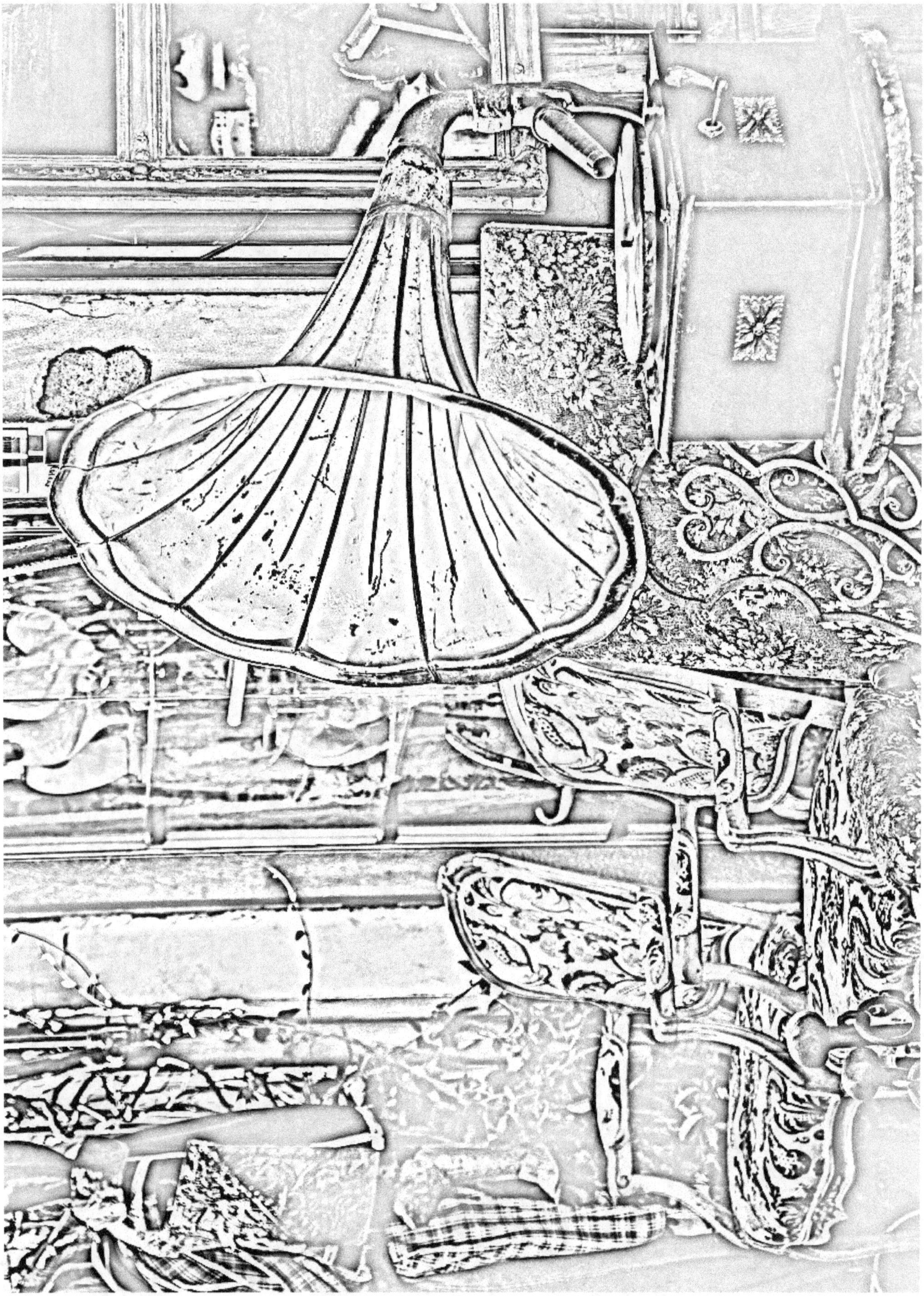

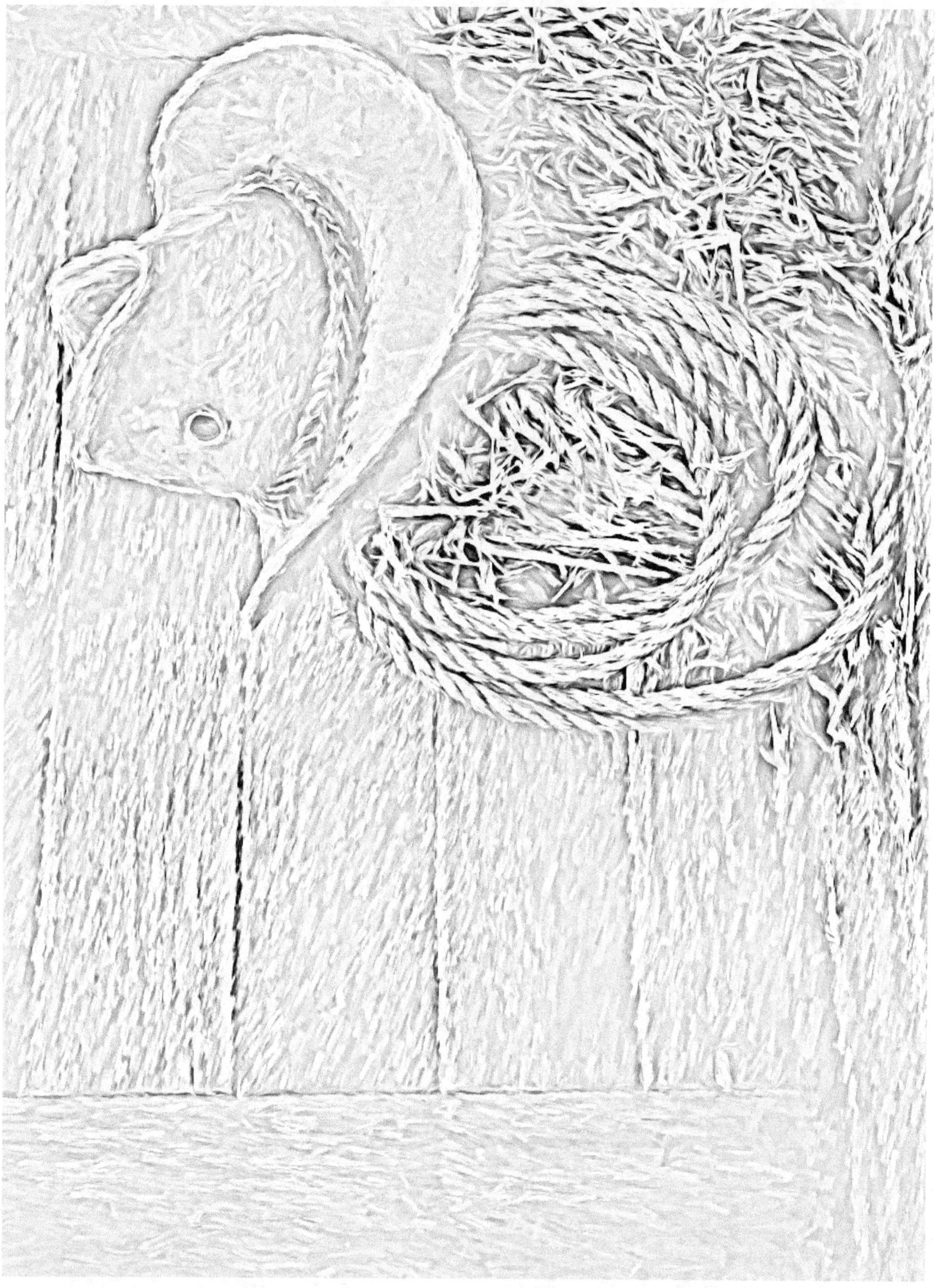

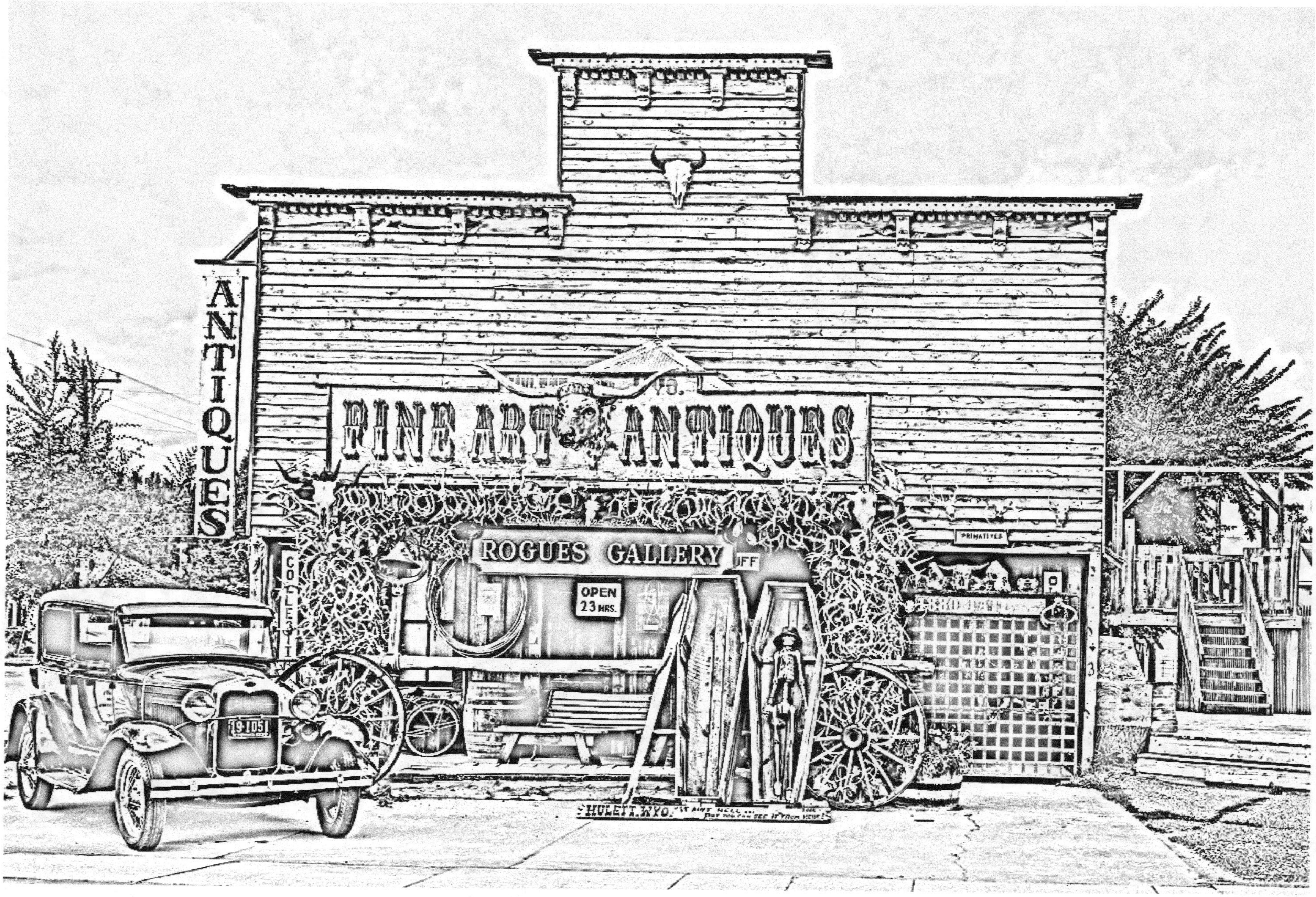
ANTIQUES
FINE ART ANTIQUES
ROGUES GALLERY
OPEN
23 HRS.
PRIMATIVES
19-105
HULETT, WYO.

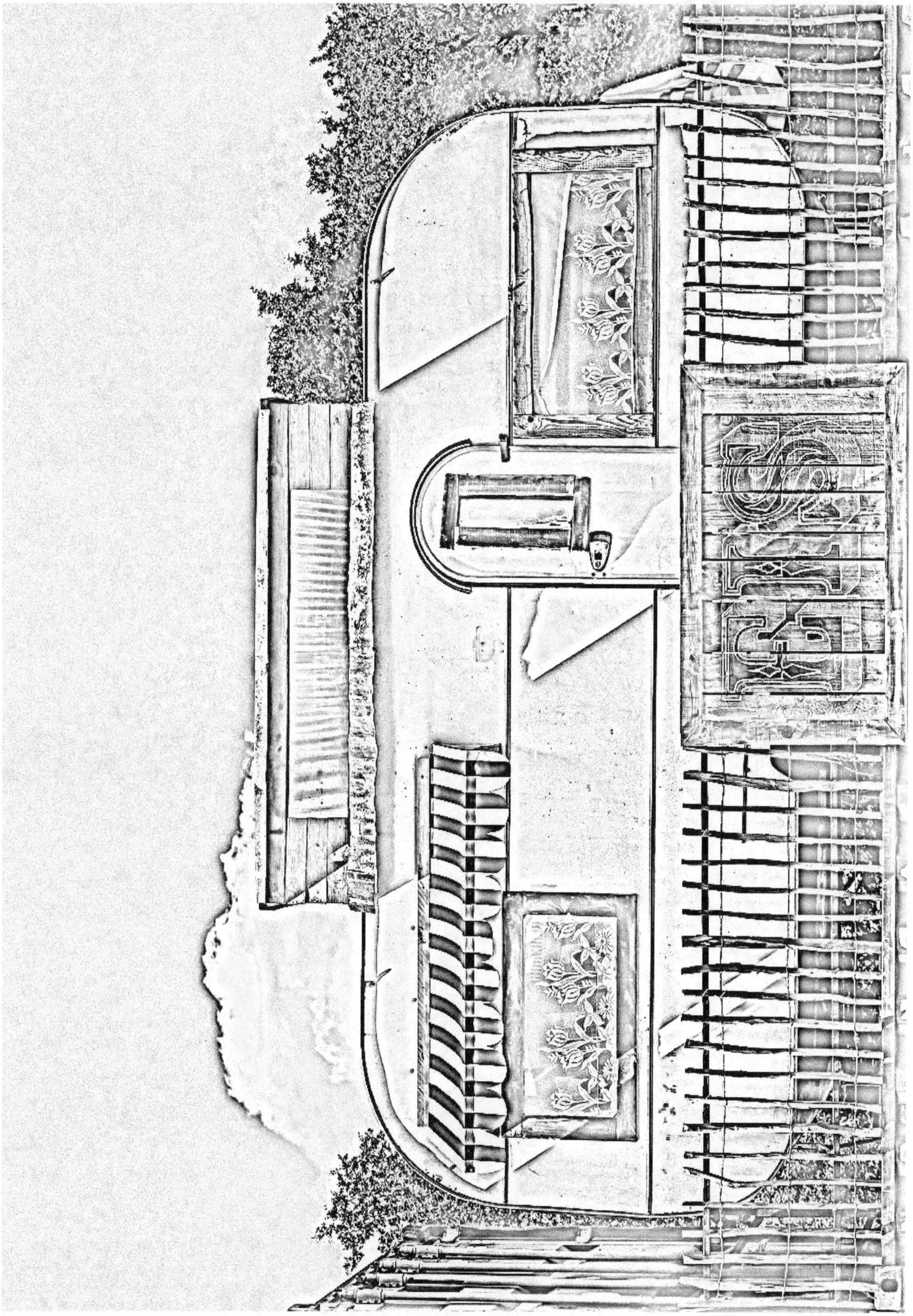

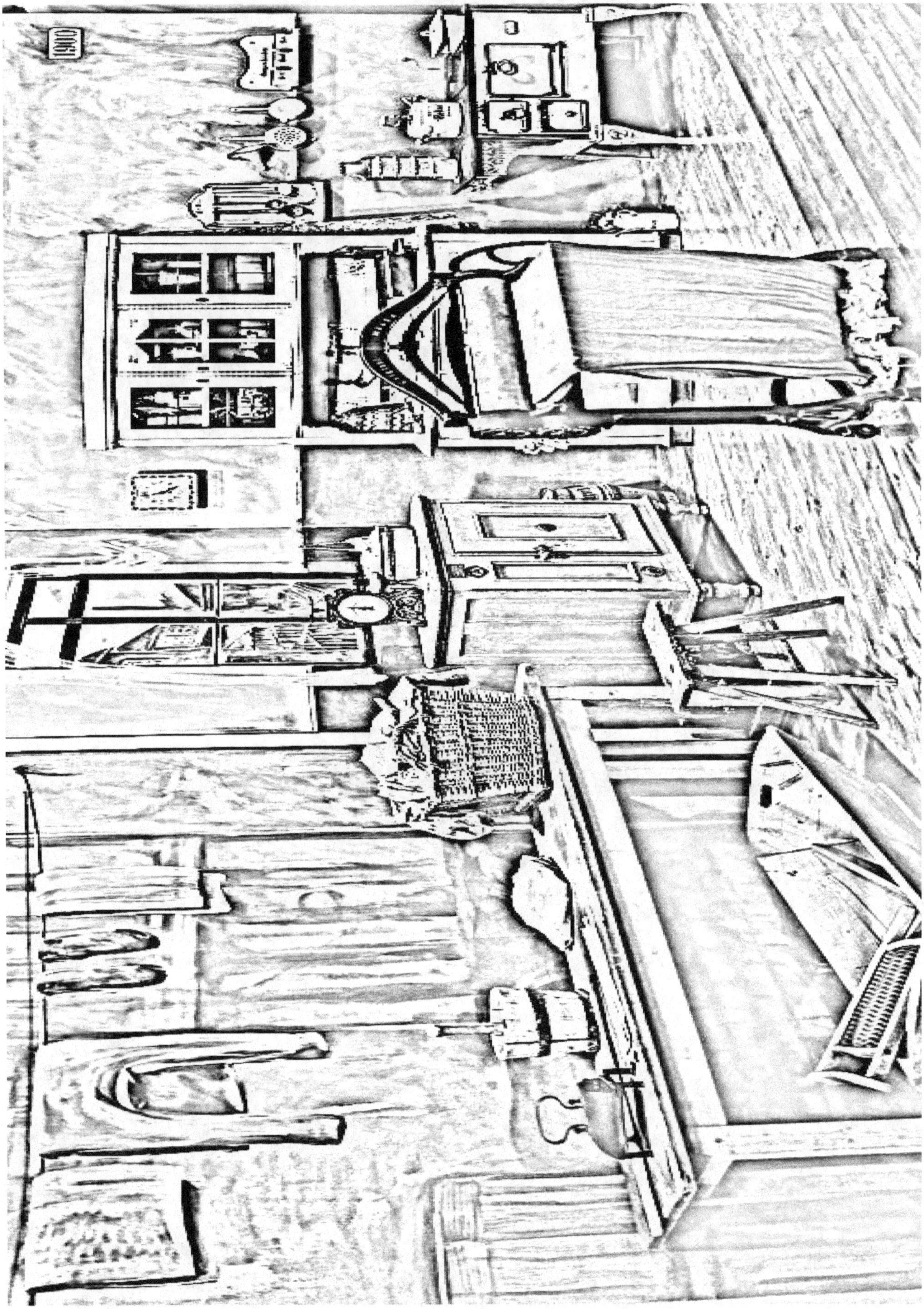

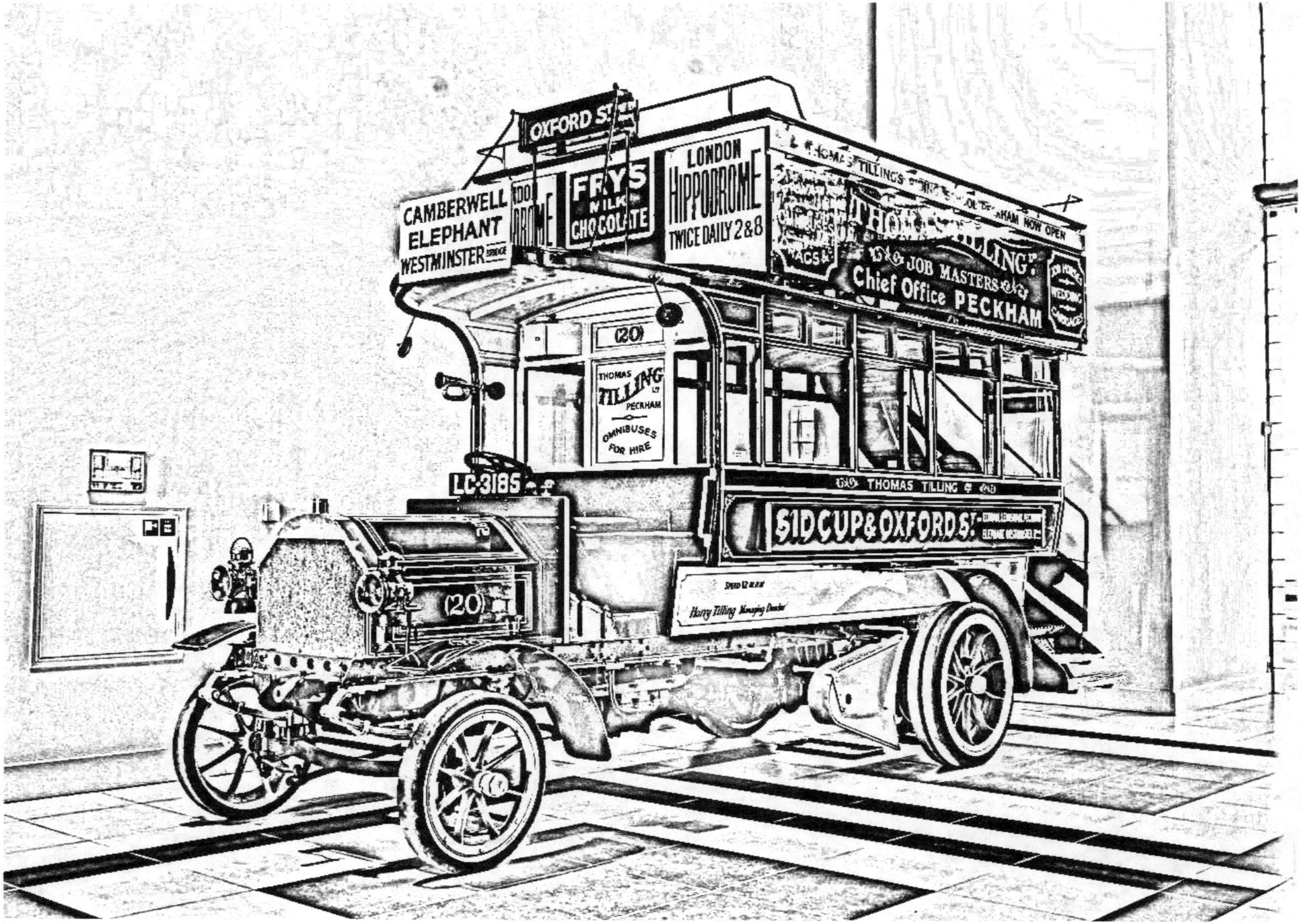
OXFORD ST.
CAMBERWELL
ELEPHANT
WESTMINSTER BRIDGE
FRYS
MILK
CHOCOLATE
LONDON
HIPPODROME
TWICE DAILY 2&8
JOB MASTERS
Chief Office PECKHAM
(20)
THOMAS
TILLING
PECKHAM
OMNIBUSES
FOR HIRE
LC-3185
THOMAS TILLING
SIDCUP&OXFORD ST.
(20)

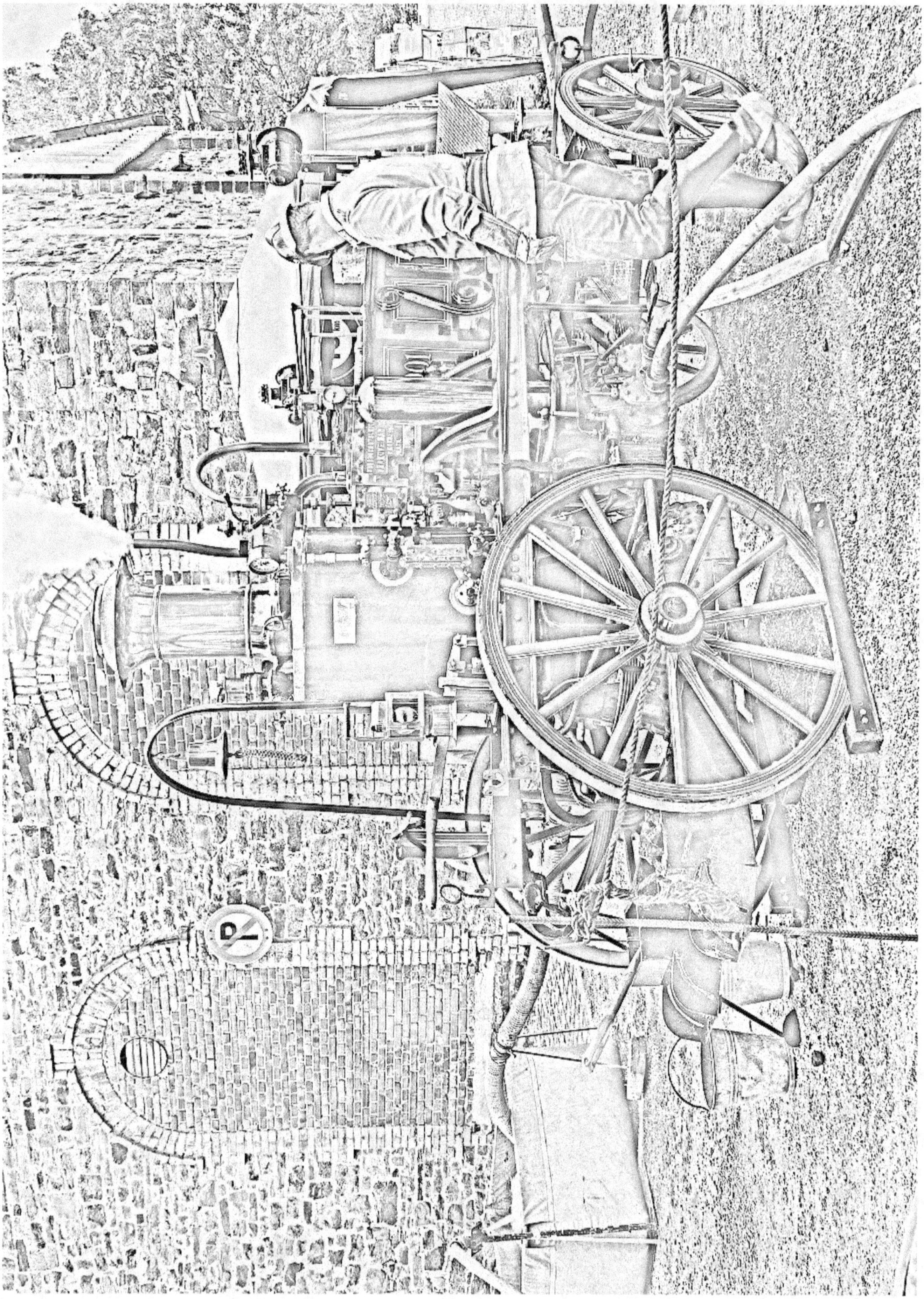

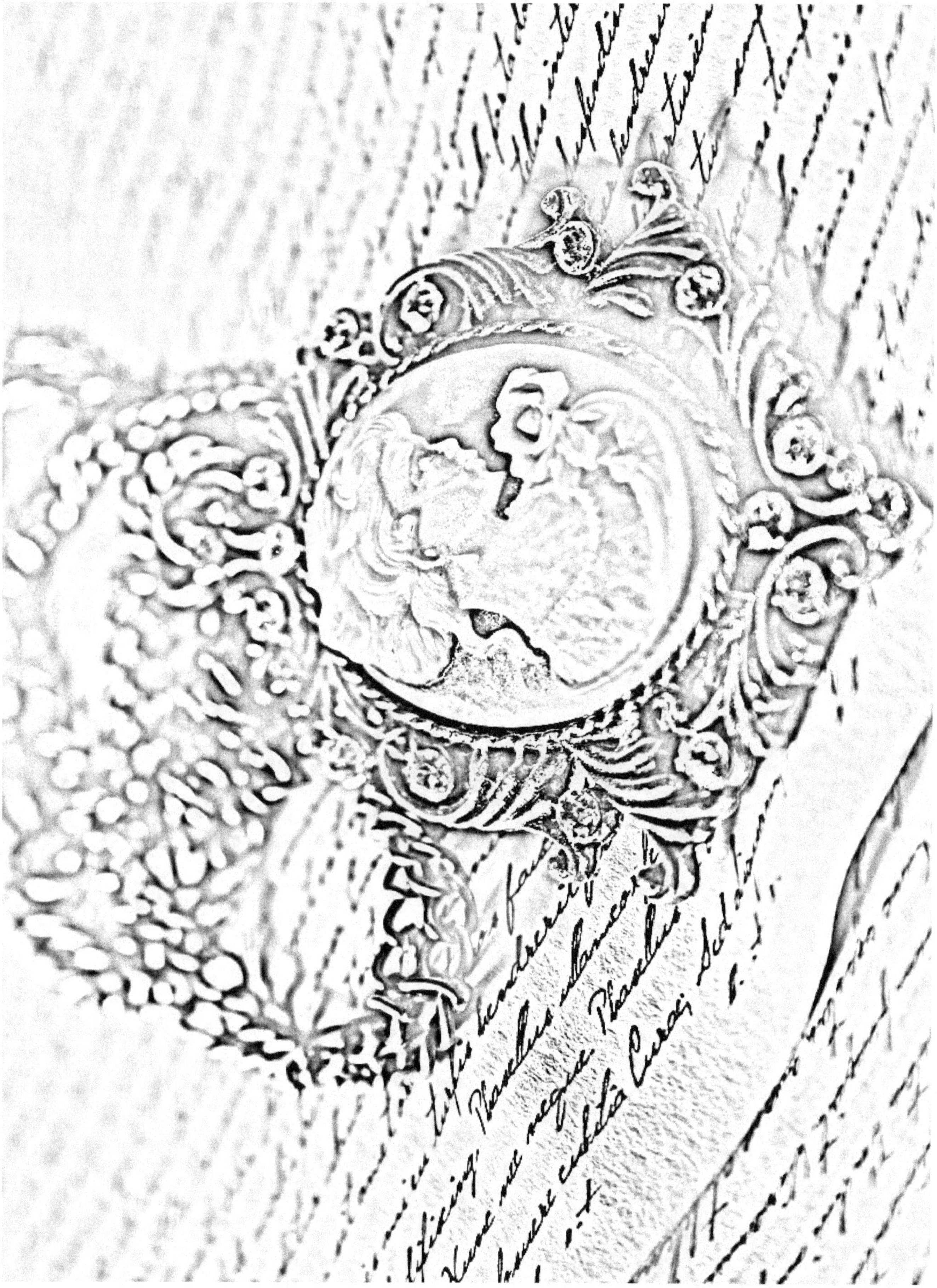

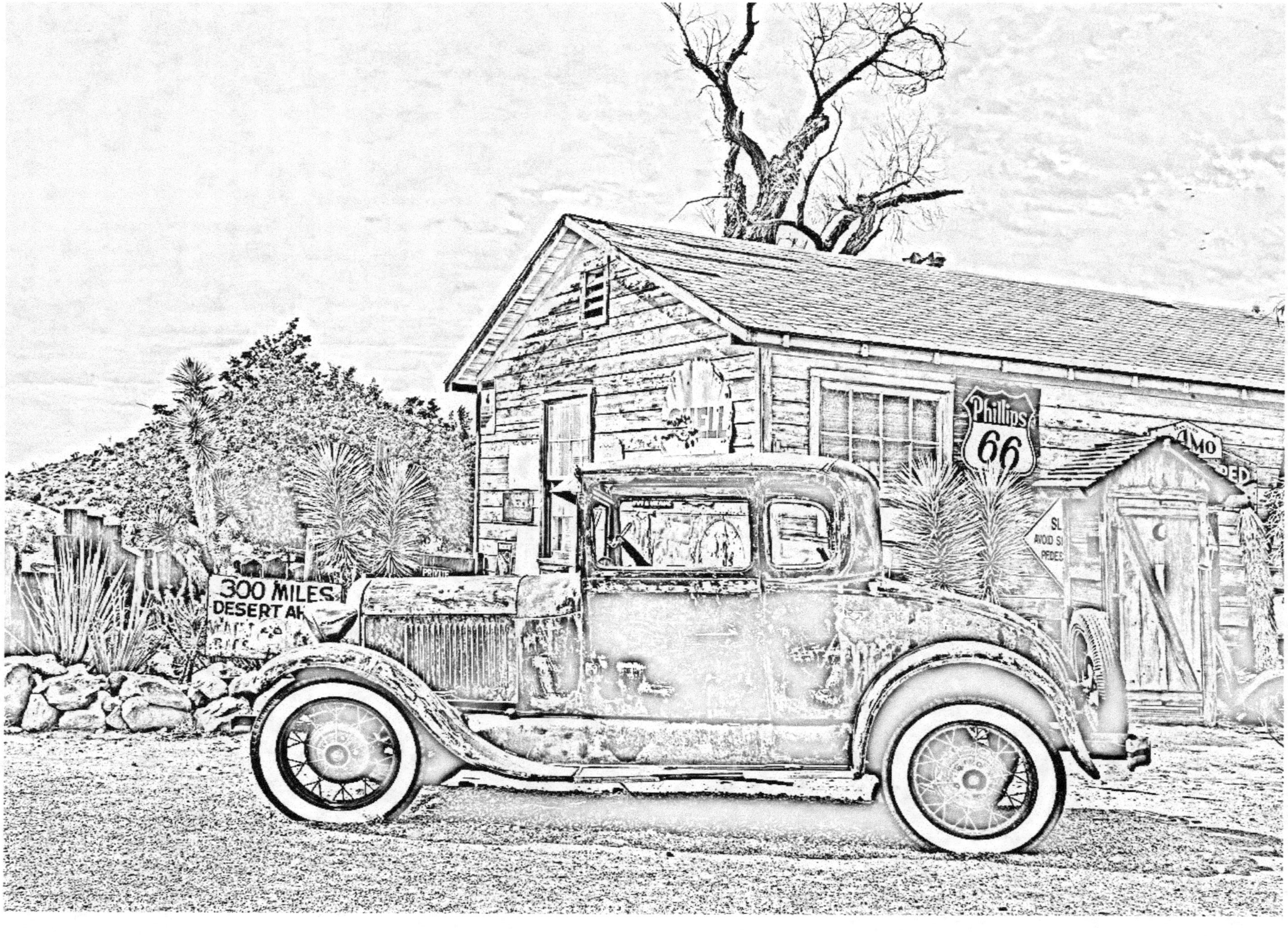
Phillips
66
300 MILES
DESERT AH
SHELL

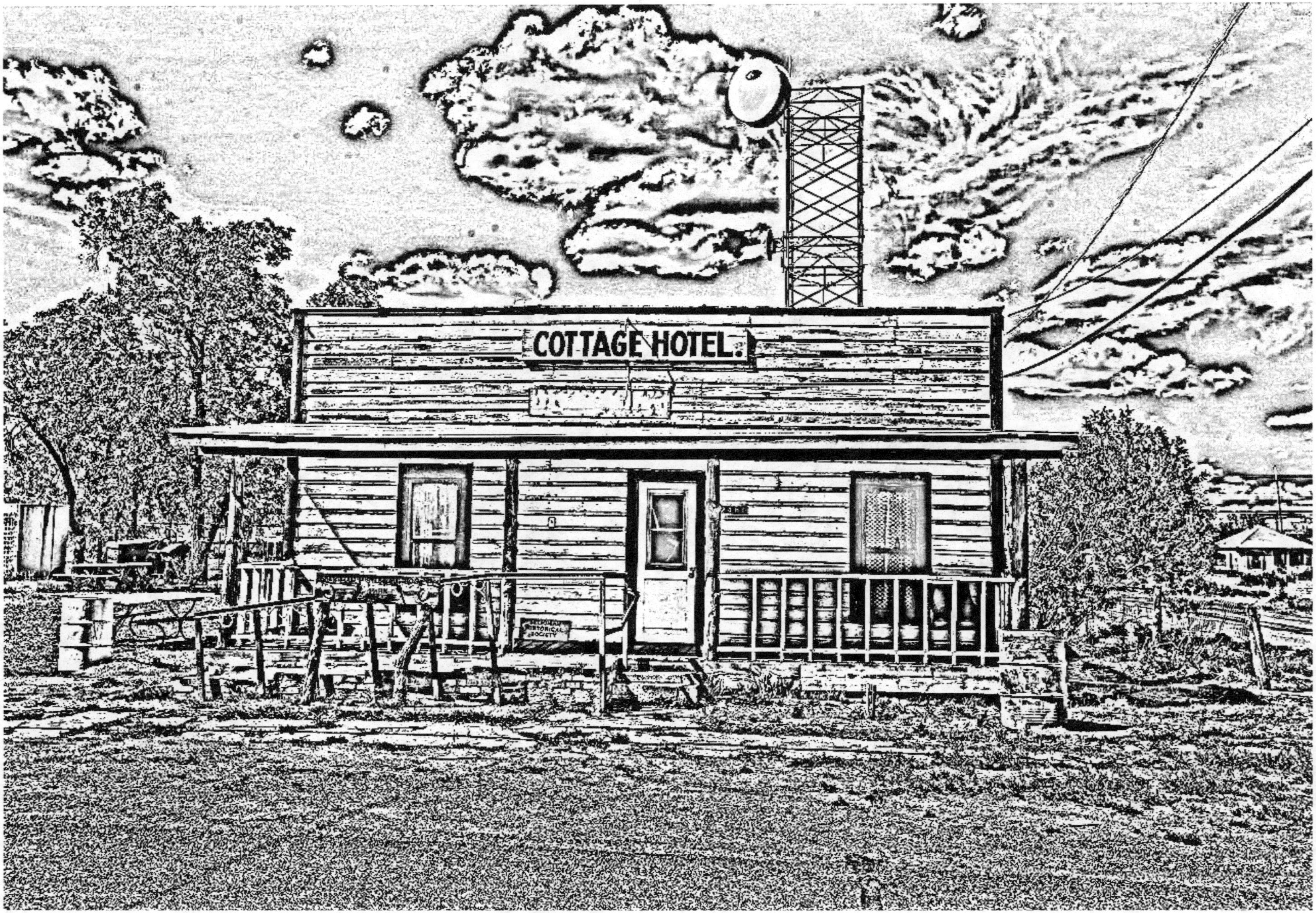
COTTAGE HOTEL.

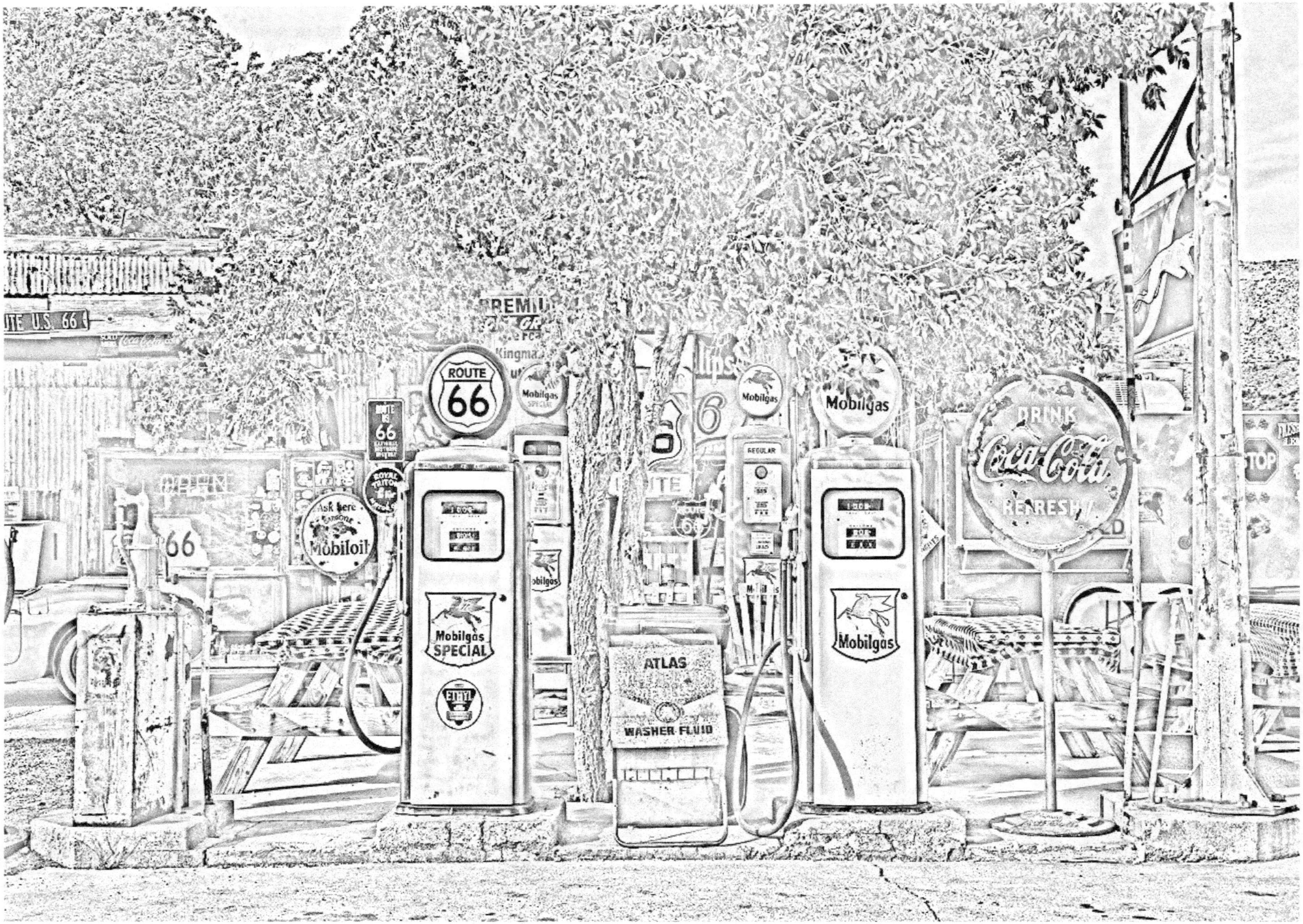
ROUTE
66
Mobilgas
Mobilgas
SPECIAL
Mobilgas
Mobilgas
REGULAR
DRINK
Coca-Cola
ATLAS
WASHER FLUID
Mobiloil
STOP

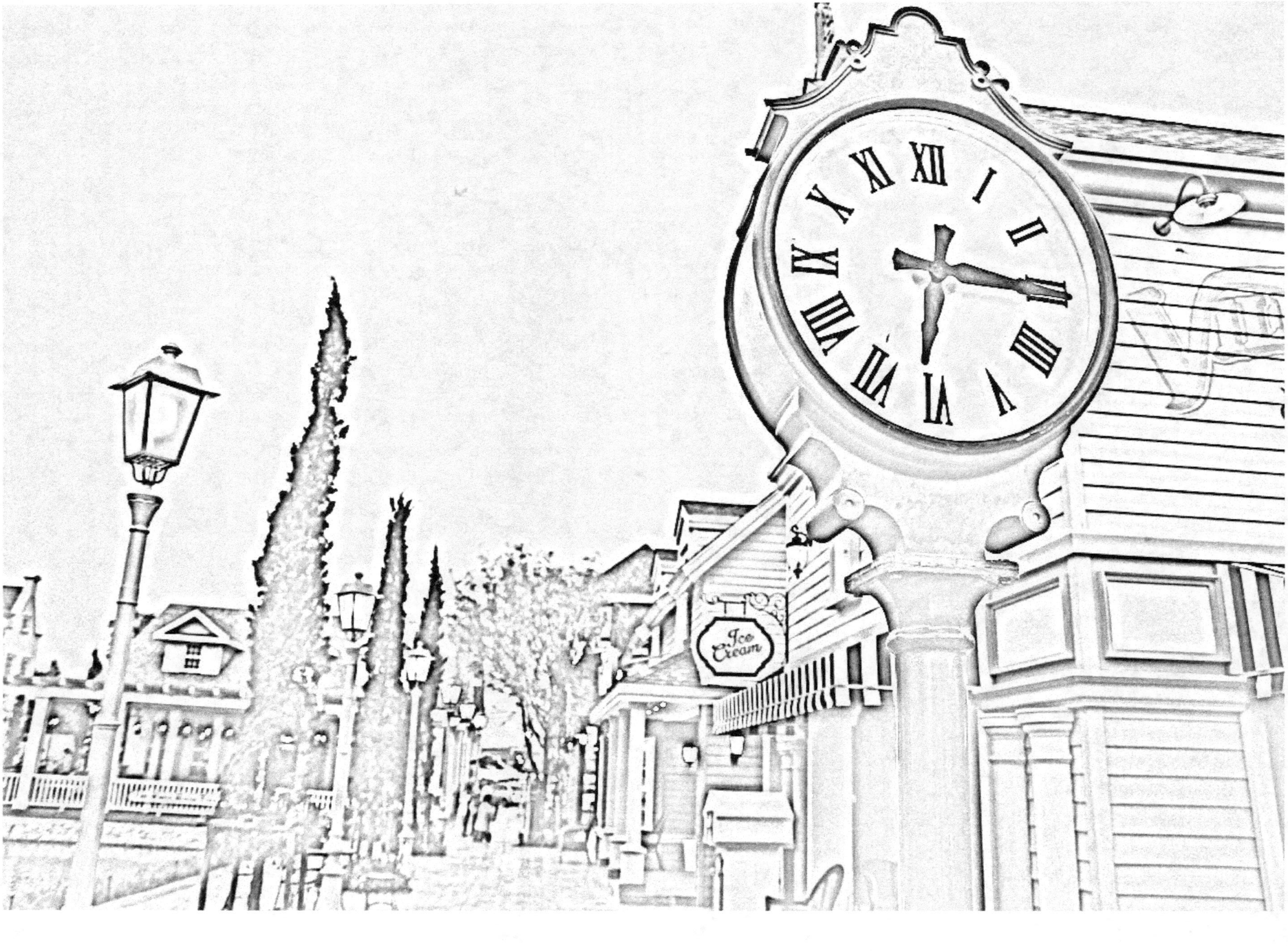
Ice Cream

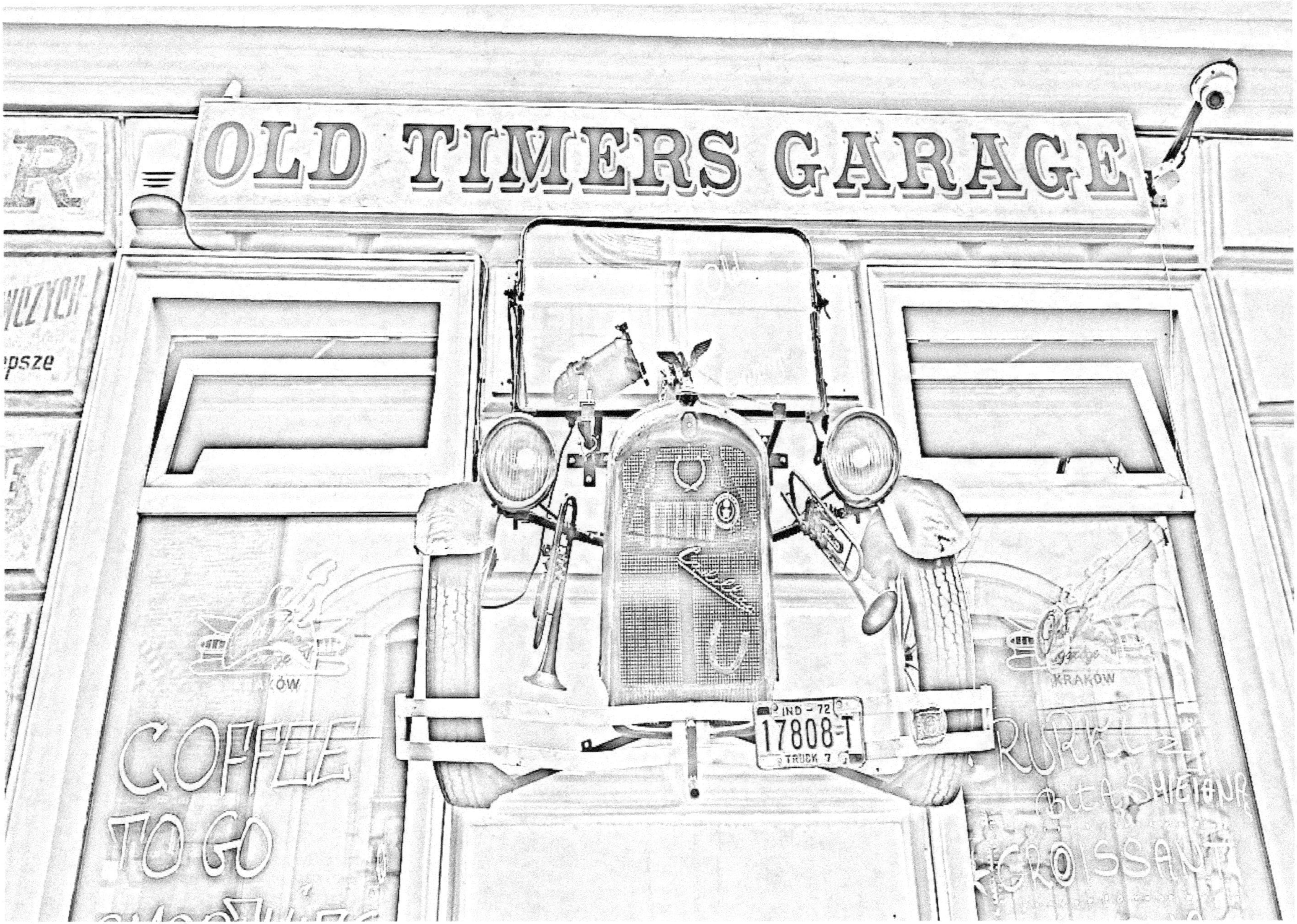
OLD TIMERS GARAGE
COFFEE
TO GO
KRAKÓW
IND - 72
17808-T
TRUCK 7
CROISSANT

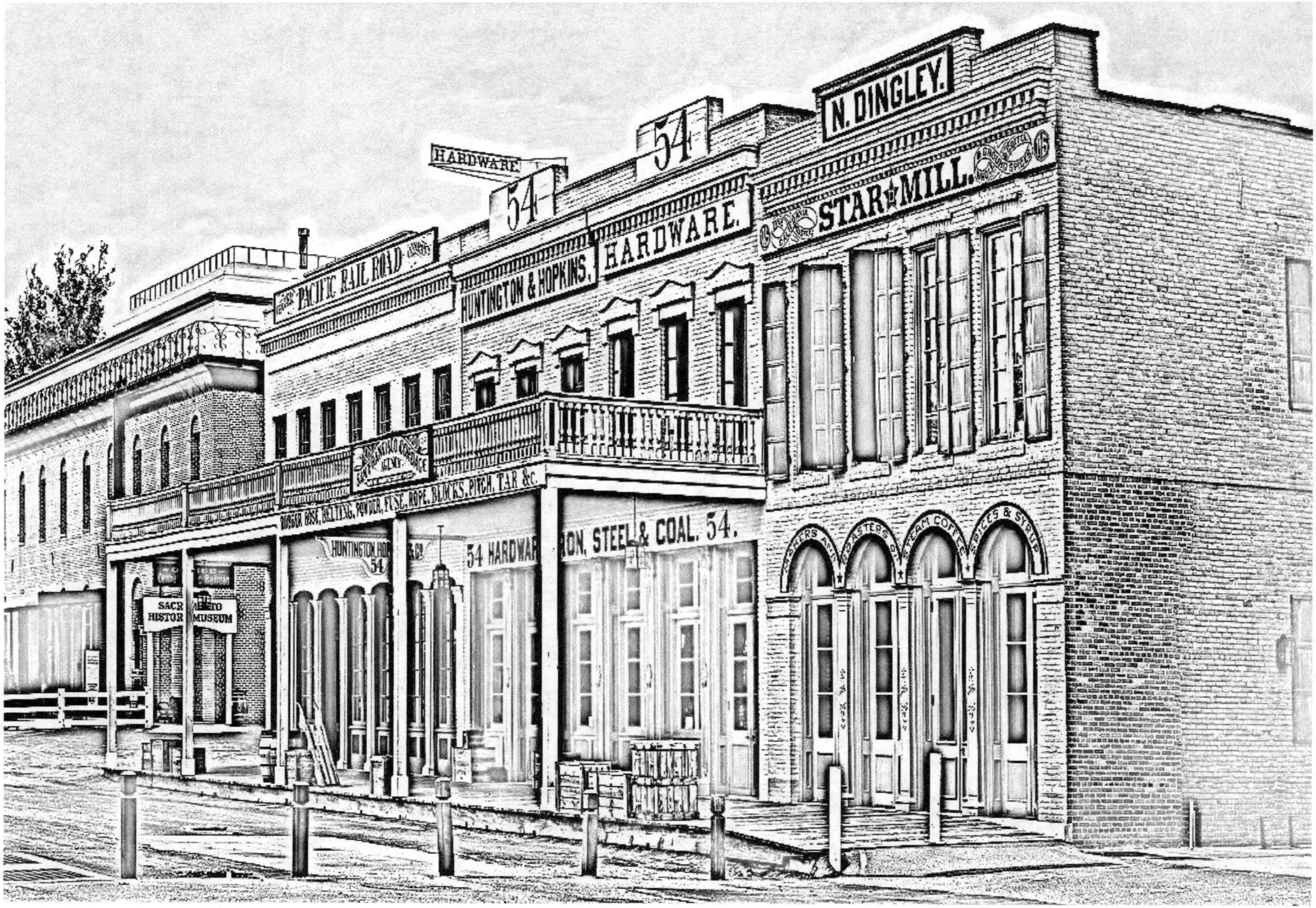
N. DINGLEY.
STAR MILL.
54
HARDWARE
54
HARDWARE.
HUNTINGTON & HOPKINS,
PACIFIC RAIL ROAD
RUBBER HOSE, BELTING, POWDER, FUSE, ROPE, BLOCKS, PITCH, TAR &c.
54 HARDWAR
RON, STEEL & COAL. 54.
SACR
HISTOR
MUSEUM

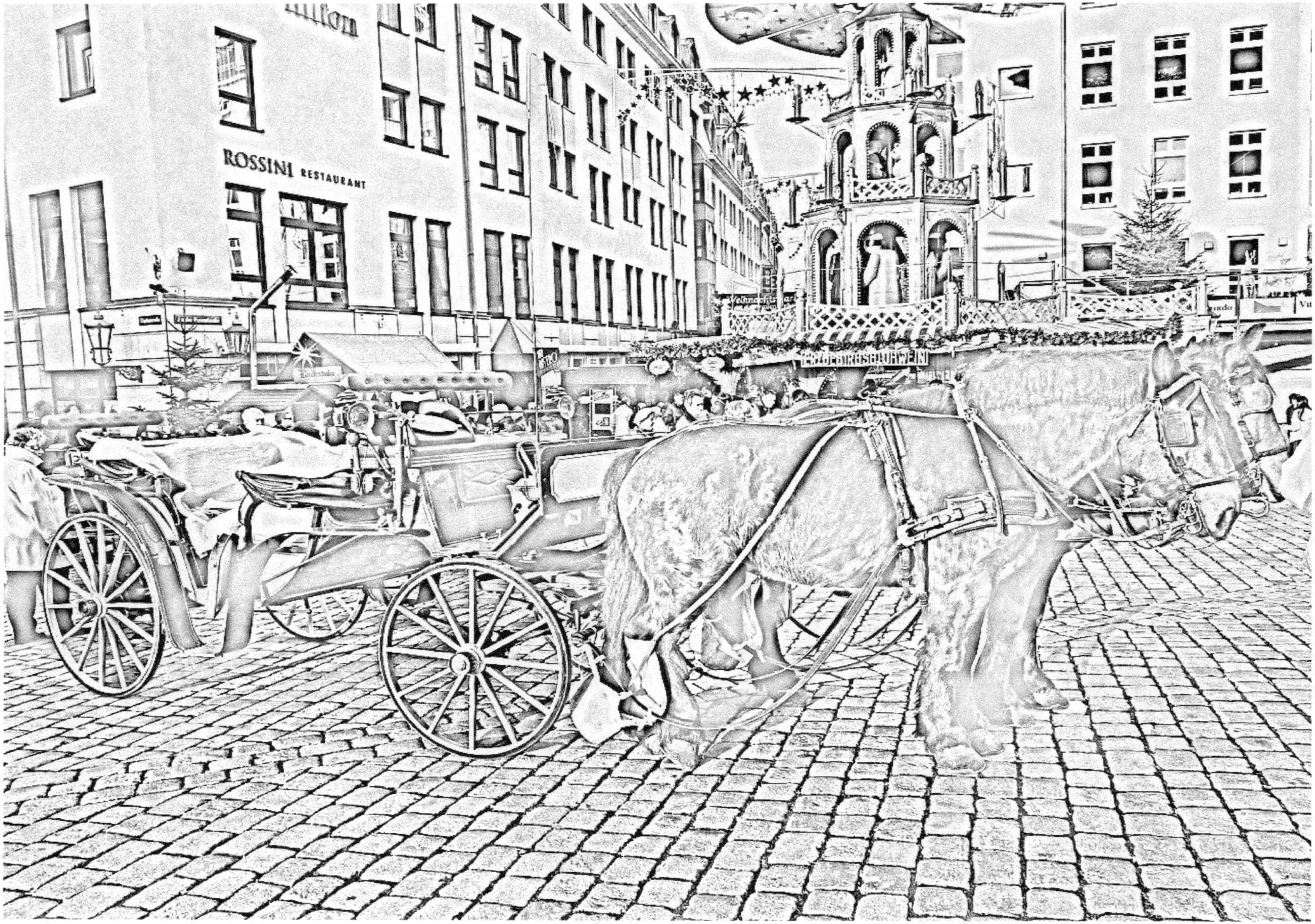
ROSSINI RESTAURANT

Thank You!

We hope you enjoyed our coloring book.

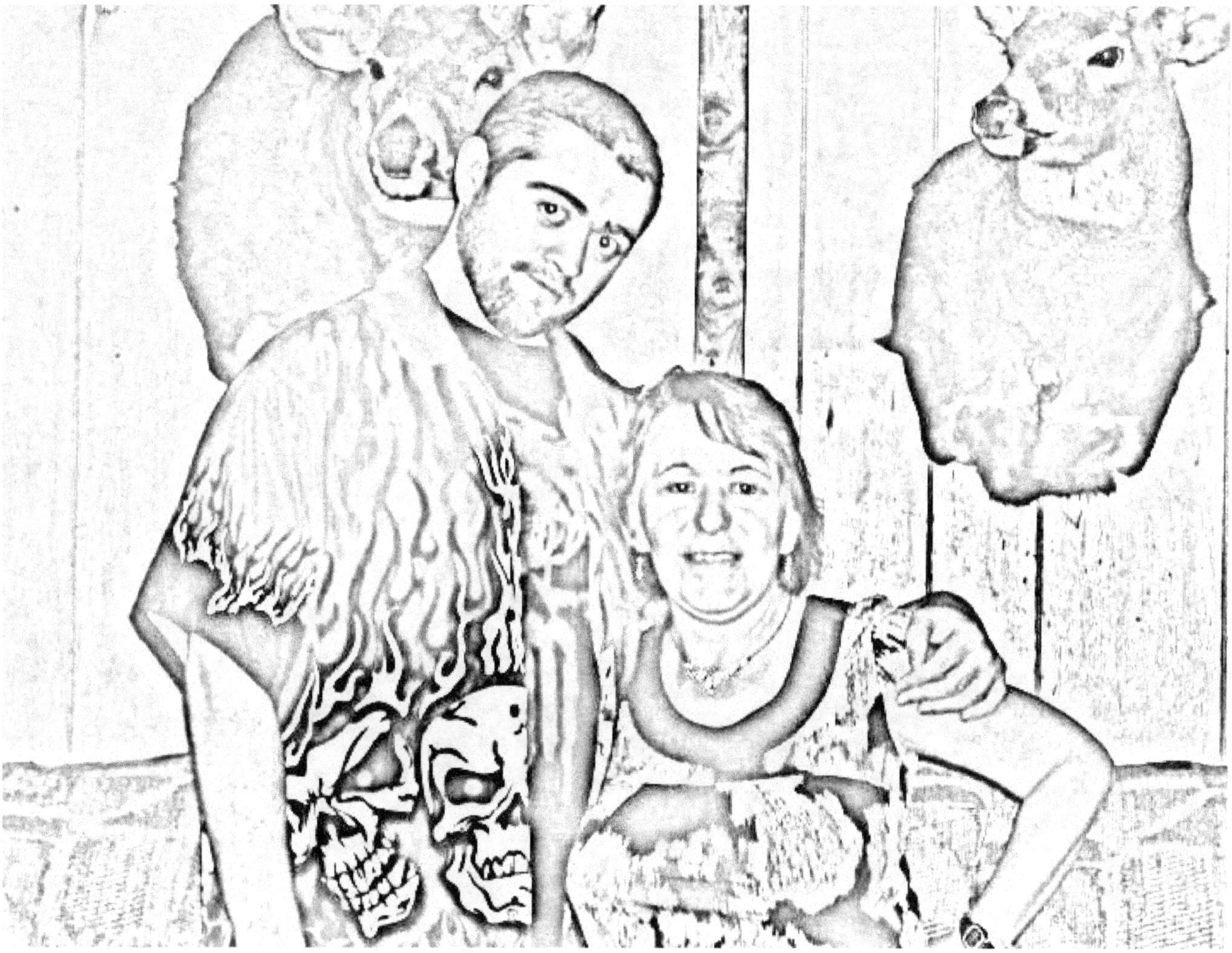

Watch for more color books from ARN Arts LLC.

You can visit http://arnarts.wixsite.com/books.

www.ingramcontent.com/pod-product-compliance
Lightning Source LLC
Chambersburg PA
CBHW081125180526
45170CB00008B/3002